DOING
UNTO OTHERS

The Patterns of Social Behavior series
Zick Rubin, *Harvard University, General Editor*

This series brings both psychological and sociological perspectives to bear on the ways in which people affect one another. Each volume explores research on a particular aspect of social behavior and considers its personal and social implications.

ZICK RUBIN is Lecturer on Social Psychology in the Department of Psychology and Social Relations at Harvard University. He received his BA in psychology from Yale University in 1965 and his PhD in social psychology from the University of Michigan in 1969. He was awarded the 1969 Socio-Psychological Prize of the American Association for the Advancement of Science for his research on the social psychology of romantic love. Dr. Rubin's current research focuses on the development of interpersonal bonds, both in brief encounters between strangers and in long-term relationships. He is author of *Liking and Loving: An Invitation to Social Psychology* (1973).

DOING UNTO OTHERS

joining
molding
conforming
helping
loving

edited by
ZICK RUBIN

PRENTICE-HALL, INC., Englewood Cliffs, New Jersey

Library of Congress Cataloging in Publication Data
RUBIN, ZICK, comp.
Doing unto others.

(Patterns of social behavior) (A Spectrum Book)
Includes bibliographical references.
CONTENTS: Schachter, S. The psychology of affiliation.—Weiss, R. S. The provisions of social relationships.—Kanter, R. M. 'Getting it all together'. [etc.]
1. Interpersonal relations—Addresses, essays, lecturers. I. Title.
HM132.R85 1974 301.11 74-32424
ISBN 0-13-217604-1
ISBN 0-13-217596-7 pbk.

A SPECTRUM BOOK

10 9 8 7 6 5 4 3 2 1

Printed in the United States of America

PRENTICE-HALL INTERNATIONAL, INC. (*London*)
PRENTICE-HALL OF AUSTRALIA PTY., LTD. (*Sydney*)
PRENTICE-HALL OF CANADA, LTD. (*Toronto*)
PRENTICE-HALL OF INDIA PRIVATE LIMITED (*New Delhi*)
PRENTICE-HALL OF JAPAN, INC. (*Tokyo*)

Contents

HELPING 111

LOVING 133

DOING UNTO OTHERS

INTRODUCTION: DOING UNTO OTHERS

We devote most of our lives to doing unto others—and being done unto in return. We join one another in pairs, groups, and organizations. We mold one another's behavior through subtle and not-so-subtle messages. We conform to the opinions and demands of others. We help one another in times of need. We experience and express love for one another.

Joining, molding, conforming, helping, and loving do not fully exhaust the ways in which people relate to one another. Each social coin has its opposite side as well. Thus we may also speak of separating, resisting, hurting, and hating. (There is no simple term for the opposite side of "molding," perhaps attesting to its pervasiveness in human affairs.) There are still other varieties of doing unto others: for example, praising and blaming, disclosing and concealing, accepting and rejecting. If viewed broadly, however, the five themes of this book encompass a large proportion of human social interaction. As such, they provide a framework for examining a broad spectrum of the contemporary field of social psychology.

As the selections in this book will demonstrate, the five themes of doing unto others are highly interrelated. We seek to join with others in order to obtain resources that only other people can provide, and our success in establishing interpersonal ties is perhaps the most important determinant of our psychological well-being. Joining is, moreover, an essential precondition for the rest of social life. Thus an understanding of the joining process—the nature of human affiliation, pairing, and group formation—is necessary for a full understanding of social interaction.

Almost as soon as people come into contact with one another, starting with the earliest interactions between infants and their parents, the molding process begins. Each of us sends and receives signals about expected and desirable patterns of behavior. These expectations are further codified into patterns of norms and roles which effectively shape much of our behavior. A more technical term often used for the molding process is "socialization."

Conforming is a central aspect of the molding process. The groups to which we belong wield tremendous power over our opinions and actions, serving both as arbiters of right and wrong and as dispensers of approval and disapproval. Without conformity, social life would be chaos. But people are also likely to conform too much, abandoning their own better judgment in order to "go along with the group."

Helping often follows from molding and conforming. We are taught at home and at school that we should help others who are in need. The Golden Rule—"Do unto others as you would have them do unto you" (also known to social scientists as the "norm of reciprocity")—exemplifies a socially approved standard of helping. In many cases, however, social roles and pressures serve to inhibit helping and instead promote apathy.

Loving is in part an amalgam of joining and helping. We typically want to be in the presence of a loved one and feel special concern for the loved one's well-being. Loving is related to molding and conforming as well. Among the most important social messages that we receive, from early childhood on, concern whom and how we should love.

Because of the many interconnections among these five themes, a single action may often represent two or more of the themes simultaneously. A parent who bestows praise and affection on a child for behaving like "a good little boy" or "a good little girl" is at once both loving and molding. An employee who succumbs to appeals to take part in his company's blood drive is simultaneously conforming and helping. Sorority pinning rituals and traditional marriage ceremonies include elements of joining, conforming, and loving. The themes combine with one another, sometimes in harmony and sometimes in discord, to produce the grand symphony of social interaction.

The attempt to understand the ways in which people do unto others is valuable for several reasons. Part of it is sheer curiosity. There is a strong human motive to explore the world around us, and this motive extends to the social environment quite as much as the physical. In addition, the exploration of patterns of social interaction may help us to come to terms with the problems and uncertainties that pervade social life. At a time of rapid geographical and social mobility, for example, the processes of making friends and establishing communities are often beset with difficulties. As we begin to question some of the traditional roles and institutions of our society, such as those related to gender, the process of molding itself becomes one of central importance. Conformity has also become a special concern as we observe soldiers obeying illegitimate orders and White House policy makers falling victim to "groupthink." Both the hectic urban environment and the "do your own thing" philosophy often seem to stand opposed to interpersonal involvement and helping. And with the fading of certain conventional standards of courtship and marriage, many people are terribly confused about loving. Research that sheds light on the basic themes of social behavior may help us to deal with these difficulties. Sometimes the ways in which people affect others seem to be undesirable or demeaning. In such cases, a systematic understanding of the underlying processes is a prerequisite for an individual's intelligent attempt to alter these patterns.

Throughout history, people have been concerned with explaining patterns of social behavior. But their attempts to do so have generally been confined to casual observation and armchair philosophy. It is only recently that our attempts to understand these patterns have turned to systematic investigation. The birth of social psychology as a scientific discipline took place at about the beginning of the present century, and the vast bulk of social-psychological research has been conducted in the years since World War II. The fourteen selections included in this book are even more recent than that. All but four of them (the papers by Schachter, Asch, Milgram, and Goode) were written since 1968.

The papers in this book include a good deal of theorizing and speculation about patterns of social behavior, but all of them remain grounded in systematic empirical research. The particular research tools employed are varied. They include historical and cross-cultural analyses (Kanter, Janis, Goode), survey and interview studies (Weiss, Fellner-Marshall, Rubin), systematic observation of behavior (Henley), laboratory experiments (Schachter, Asch, Milgram, Latané-Darley, Walster), and experiments conducted outside the laboratory (Rosenthal-Jacobson, Zimbardo, et al.).

These papers were selected, from a much wider range of possibilities, with several criteria in mind. Most importantly, I wanted to include work that has shed real light on the five themes of doing unto others. Some of the papers are better known among social psychologists than others, including several that are recognized as classic contributions. All of them, however, have been influential in prompting further research into patterns of social behavior. I also tried to include work that represented a wide range of approaches toward social interaction, from the "psychological" to the "sociological," and especially the rich interface between these two levels of analysis. Some of the writers are identified primarily as "psychologists," some as "sociologists," and some with still other disciplines. Many (perhaps most) of them are strongly drawn to an interdisciplinary approach, and would prefer to be identified as "social psychologists." Finally, the papers were chosen for their readability, in my determined effort to demonstrate that empirically oriented social scientists can write after all.

• • •

To return to the theme of helping, I am grateful to the authors of the papers in this book for permission to include them, and in several cases for undertaking revisions or preparing new material for the occasion. I also want to thank Michael Hunter, Cyndi Mitchell, and Carol Rubin for their assistance in the planning and preparation of the book.

JOINING

People are joiners. We are born into families, play with friends, attend schools, crowd into subways, join together in marriage, congregate in churches, live in neighborhoods, work for organizations, and retire in planned communities. We seek ties with others when it seems objectively necessary to do so, but also when it does not. Yet there are also times when we renounce interpersonal ties and seek solitude.

Before people can interact in any other ways, they must first get together. Therefore, an understanding of how and why joining takes place is a prerequisite to a further understanding of patterns of social behavior. The three selections in this section address themselves to three fundamental questions about human affiliation: First, why do people seek the company of others? Second, what are the functions served by interpersonal relationships? And third, how do groups of people get together—and stay together?

Stanley Schachter addresses himself to the first of these questions, focusing on the anxiety-reducing effects of human affiliation. His pioneering experiment demonstrated that humans, like other animals, are particularly likely to seek one another's company when they are afraid or anxious. In his subsequent research Schachter proceeded to go beyond the demonstration that "Misery loves company" to a more precise account of when and why this is the case. He concluded that a central source of human gregariousness is the need to get help in evaluating our own feelings, abilities, and attitudes by comparing ourselves to others.

Whereas Schachter's research concerns affiliation with others in general, Robert S. Weiss has focused on the establishment of relationships with a particular other. At the heart of his work is the idea that relationships tend to be specialized in the psychological and social resources that they provide. For example, marital relationships often serve most prominently as sources of emotional sustenance and security, whereas same-sex friendships are more likely to provide opportunities for social comparison. A central insight, which Weiss has documented through intensive interview studies, is that both sorts of relationships, as well as several other sorts, are necessary for psychological well-being.

The search for community, of a sort that ideally can make available several of the provisions that Weiss discusses, is the starting point for Rosabeth Moss Kanter's analysis. Given that the desire to "get it all together" is present, there are many practical problems that remain to be solved before a viable group can be established. Kanter derives some valuable lessons about the creation of community from a comparison of successful and unsuccessful utopian communes of the 19th century. She then perceptively applies these lessons to the tasks facing present-day endeavors in communal living.

All three papers converge on the common themes that people join others in order to obtain important psychological resources—provisions that go far beyond material goods and services. Especially in the face of high geographical mobility and rapid social change, our need to affiliate with others is often hard to fulfill, leading to feelings of frustration or loneliness. Social-psychological analyses of affiliation do not in themselves provide solutions to these problems, but they provide an important part of the background needed by individuals and social planners in their search for solutions.

The Psychology of Affiliation

Stanley Schachter

Walt Whitman once wrote, "I . . . demand the most copious and close companionship of men." The sentiment is familiar, for most of us have experienced occasional cravings to be with people, sometimes for good reason, frequently for no apparent reason: we seem simply to want to be in the physical presence of others. Whatever the reasons, these desires that draw men together furnish the substance of the social sciences, which in good part are devoted to the study of the process and products of human association.

Despite the importance of the study of the affiliative needs, almost nothing is known of the variables and conditions affecting these needs. We have no precise idea of the circumstances that drive men either to seek one another out or to crave privacy, and we have only the vaguest and most obvious sort of suggestions concerning the kinds of satisfaction that men seek in company. A review of the literature indicates that there has been some psychoanalytic thought on the topic; that, at most, there have been two or three immediately relevant experiments; and, most prominently, that there has been a generous amount of common sense, mildly obvious formulation of the fact that people do associate.

The gist of what we have called the "common sense" line of thought may be summarized in two propositions:

First, people do mediate goals for one another, and it may be necessary to associate with other people or belong to particular groups in order to obtain specifiable individual goals. For example, to hold a job it may be necessary to join a union; to play bridge it may be necessary to become a member of a bridge club; and so on.

Second, people, in and of themselves, represent goals for one another;

Abridged from Stanley Schachter, *The Psychology of Affiliation,* pp. 1–19, with permission of the author and the publisher, Stanford University Press.

that is, people do have needs which can be satisfied *only* in interpersonal relations. Approval, support, friendship, prestige, and the like have been offered as examples of such needs. There is no doubt that such needs are particularly powerful ones and that association with other people is a necessity for most of us.

The distinction drawn in these two propositions is hardly a sharp one, and one could quibble endlessly as to whether this is a distinction at all. The relative emphasis of the two propositions, however, is clear enough. In the one case, association represents a means to an essentially asocial goal; in the other, the gratifications, whatever they may be, of association itself represent the goal. It is our intention to concentrate on the latter type of associational activity and to attempt to spell out some of the circumstances and variables affecting the affiliative tendencies.

THE NEED FOR SELF-EVALUATION

One set of needs that may be satisfiable only by association with other people is discussed by Festinger in his theoretical paper on social comparison processes. Festinger writes:

> The drive for self evaluation concerning one's opinions and abilities has implications not only for the behavior of persons in groups but also for the processes of formation of groups and changing membership of groups. To the extent that self evaluation can only be accomplished by means of comparison with other persons, the drive for self evaluation is a force acting on persons to belong to groups, to associate with others. And the subjective feelings of correctness in one's opinions and the subjective evaluation of adequacy of one's performance on important abilities are some of the satisfactions that persons attain in the course of these associations with other people. How strong the drives and satisfactions stemming from these sources are compared to the other needs which people satisfy in groups is impossible to say, but it seems clear that the drive for self evaluation is an important factor contributing to making the human being "gregarious." [1]

Though the assumption of a drive for evaluation of the opinions and abilities has proven particularly fruitful in generating research tests of its implications, whether or not such a drive is indeed a major source of "gregariousness" is still an open question, however, for there are, unfortunately, almost no studies bearing directly on the question. The single piece of research that is relevant is the case study by Festinger, Riecken, and Schachter[2] of a millenial group. This group had predicted, for a specific date, the destruction of the world as we know it through a series

[1] L. Festinger, "A theory of social comparison processes," *Human Relations*, 1954, *7*, 117–140.

[2] L. Festinger, H. Riecken, and S. Schachter, *When Prophecy Fails* (Minneapolis: University of Minnesota Press, 1956).

of earth-shaking cataclysms—a prediction which was not confirmed. The effect of this disconfirmation was, of course, to shake all confidence in the belief system which had led to this prediction. The almost immediate reaction to disconfirmation was a frenzy of attempts to convert and proselyte. Prior to disconfirmation, this group had been secretive and inhospitable, avoiding all publicity and contact with outsiders. Following disconfirmation, they exposed themselves to the world, called in newspapers, and worked furiously to convince possible converts—all, presumably, in an attempt to establish a new and firm social basis for their beliefs.

If one broadens this "drive for evaluation of opinions and abilities" into a more general "drive for cognitive clarity," one does find additional evidence for the proposition that evaluative or cognitive needs are an important source of affiliative behavior. There are many thoroughly ambiguous issues that are impossible to clarify by reference either to the physical world or to authoritative sources. For such issues, if one assumes a need for cognitive clarity, it is plausible to assume that attempts to reduce ambiguity will take the direction of intensive social contact and discussion. Evidence that this is indeed the case can be found as a byproduct of a study of rumor transmission conducted by Schachter and Burdick.[3] This study took place in a girls' school. In a deliberate attempt to create an event that would be mystifying and not readily explainable, the principal of the school went into several classrooms during first-hour classes, pointed at a single girl, and said, "Miss K., get your hat, coat, and books and come with me. You will be gone for the rest of the day." Nothing of this sort had ever occurred before and absolutely no explanation was offered. Not surprisingly, the remaining girls spent almost all of the school day in intensive social contact and communication in an attempt to clear up and understand what had happened.

Such is the research literature that has most immediately stimulated our interest in the topic—a handful of studies suggesting that people will seek one another out when their opinions are shaken and that an otherwise uninterpretable event leads to a search for social reality. Several other studies suggest that association may lead to a state of relative anonymity allowing the satisfaction of needs which might otherwise remain unsatisfied. These are intriguing leads, but it is clear that our knowledge of conditions affecting affiliative behavior is still rudimentary.

SOCIAL ISOLATION

If such evidence is needed, an examination of the consequences of social isolation shows convincingly that the social needs are indeed powerful

[3] S. Schachter and H. Burdick, "A field experiment on rumor transmission and distortion," *Journal of Abnormal and Social Psychology*, 1955, *50*, 363–371.

ones. Autobiographical reports of such people as religious hermits, prisoners of war, and castaways make it clear that the effects of isolation can be devastating. For example, a prisoner writes, "Gradually the loneliness closed in. Later on I was to experience situations which amounted almost to physical torture, but even that seemed preferable to absolute isolation." [4] Such reports are extremely common and seem to be as typical of those who have gone into voluntary isolation as of those forced into solitary confinement.

Aside from these reports of profound disturbance, anxiety, and pain, the condition of absolute social deprivation as described in these autobiographical reminiscences seems responsible for many other dramatic effects. Most prominently, the following three trends characterize many of these reports:

First, the reported "pain" of the isolation experience seems typically to bear a nonmonotonic relationship to time—increasing to a maximum and then, in many cases, decreasing sharply. This decrease in pain is frequently marked by onset of a state of apathy sometimes so severe as to resemble a schizophrenic-like state of withdrawal and detachment, so marked in some cases that prisoners have to be physically removed from their cells. Indeed, this condition is so common that the Church recognizes the state of acedia (or sloth, one of the seven deadly sins) as an occupational disease of hermits.

Second, there seems to be a strong tendency for those in isolation to think, dream, and occasionally hallucinate about people. Indeed, comparison of the anchoritic or hermit saints with the cenobitic saints indicates greater frequency of visions and hallucinatory experiences for the religious solitaries.

And third, those isolates who are able to keep themselves occupied with distracting activities appear to suffer less and be less prone to the state of apathy. Those prisoners who are able to invent occupations for themselves and schedule for themselves activities such as doing mental arithmetic or recalling poetry seem to bear up better under the experience than those who either think chiefly of their plight or dwell on the outside world.

Though all of this is of absorbing interest, its interpretation is thoroughly confounded by the multitude of coacting variables and the indistinguishability of cause and effect; proper investigation of these various phenomena demands direct and controlled study. Several years ago, therefore, in a preliminary attempt to examine some of the consequences of social isolation, the author conducted a small series of isolation case studies. Student volunteers, who were paid ten dollars a day, were supplied with food and locked into a windowless room for periods ranging from two to eight days. Their watches and wallets were removed and their

[4] A. Weissberg, *The Accused* (New York: Simon & Schuster, 1951), p. 89.

pockets emptied. Some subjects were provided with a variety of minor distracting devices, such as metal-link puzzles, dart boards, and so on. Other subjects were left completely to their own devices and entered a room barren of anything but a bed, a chair, a lamp, a table, and, unknown to the subject, a one-way observation mirror. In no case was a subject permitted books, radio, or any device that could directly serve as a social surrogate. For the period of isolation, all subjects were left completely to their own resources to spend their time as they would and with absolutely no communication with the experimenter or the outside world. In addition to these voluntary isolates, interviews were conducted with a few prisoners who, as punishment, were in solitary confinement cells at the Minnesota State Prison.

After the extremes of the autobiographical reports, this first-hand contact was sobering. The prisoners, who had been in solitary confinement for periods ranging from three to five days, were not particularly troubled by the experience; they were interested chiefly in bumming cigarettes and complaining about the food. As for the students, five subjects were run in the experimental isolation room. One subject broke down after two hours, almost hammering down the door to get out. Of three subjects who remained in isolation for a two-day period, one admitted that he had become quite uneasy and was unwilling to go through the experience again, while the other two subjects seemed quite unaffected by two days of isolation. The fifth subject was isolated for eight days. He admitted that by the end of this eight-day period he was growing uneasy and nervous, and he was certainly delighted to be able to see people again; but one could hardly describe his condition as having grown intolerable.

ANXIETY AND AFFILIATION

One of the consequences of isolation appears to be a psychological state which in its extreme form resembles a full-blown anxiety attack. In many of the autobiographical reports and in the interview protocol of our single subject who demanded his release after only two hours of confinement, there are strong indications of an overwhelming nervousness, of tremendous suffering and pain, and of a general "going-to-pieces." A milder form is illustrated by the two of our five subjects who reported that they had felt jittery, tense, and uneasy. At the other extreme, two subjects went through the experience with complete aplomb and reported no difficulties. The whole range of reactions is represented, and though we have little idea as to the variables which determine whether the reaction to isolation will be equanimity or terror, it is evident that anxiety, in some degree, is a fairly common concomitant of isolation. For a variety of frankly intuitive reasons, it seemed reasonable to expect that if conditions of isolation produce anxiety, conditions of anxiety would lead to the increase of affiliative tendencies. In order to test this proposition the following very simple experiment was constructed.

EXPERIMENTAL PROCEDURE

There were two experimental conditions, one of high anxiety and one of low anxiety. Anxiety was manipulated in the following fashion. In the high-anxiety condition, the subjects, all college girls, strangers to one another, entered a room to find facing them a gentleman of serious mien, horn-rimmed glasses, dressed in a white laboratory coat, stethoscope dribbling out of his pocket, behind him an array of formidable electrical junk. After a few preliminaries, the experimenter began:

Allow me to introduce myself, I am Dr. Gregor Zilstein of the Medical School's Departments of Neurology and Psychiatry. I have asked you all to come today in order to serve as subjects in an experiment concerned with the effects of electrical shock.

Zilstein paused ominously, then continued with a seven- or eight-minute recital of the importance of research in this area, citing electroshock therapy, the increasing number of accidents due to electricity, and so on. He concluded in this vein:

What we will ask each of you to do is very simple. We would like to give each of you a series of electric shocks. Now, I feel I must be completely honest with you and tell you exactly what you are in for. These shocks will hurt, they will be painful. As you can guess, if, in research of this sort, we're to learn anything at all that will really help humanity, it is necessary that our shocks be intense. What we will do is put an electrode on your hand, hook you into apparatus such as this [Zilstein points to the electrical-looking gadgetry behind him], give you a series of electric shocks, and take various measures such as your pulse rate, blood pressure, and so on. Again, I do want to be honest with you and tell you that these shocks will be quite painful but, of course, they will do no permanent damage.

In the low-anxiety condition, the setting and costume were precisely the same except that there was no electrical apparatus in the room. After introducing himself Zilstein proceeded:

I have asked you all to come today in order to serve as subjects in an experiment concerned with the effects of electric shock. I hasten to add, do not let the word "shock" trouble you; I am sure that you will enjoy the experiment.

Then precisely the same recital on the importance of the research, concluding with:

What we will ask each one of you to do is very simple. We would like to give each of you a series of very mild electric shocks. I assure you that what you will feel will not in any way be painful. It will resemble more a tickle or a tingle than anything unpleasant. We will put an electrode on your hand, give you a series of very mild shocks and measure such things as your pulse rate and blood pressure, measures with which I'm sure you are all familiar from visits to your family doctor.

From this point on, the experimental procedures in the two conditions were identical. In order to get a first measurement of the effectiveness of the anxiety manipulation, the experimenter continued:

Before we begin, I'd like to have you tell us how you feel about taking part in this experiment and being shocked. We need this information in order to fully understand your reactions in the shocking apparatus. I ask you therefore to be as honest as possible in answering and describe your feelings as accurately as possible.

He then passed out a sheet headed, "How do you feel about being shocked?" and asked the subjects to check the appropriate point on a five-point scale ranging from "I dislike the idea very much" to "I enjoy the idea very much."

This done, the experimenter continued:

Before we begin with the shocking proper there will be about a ten-minute delay while we get this room in order. We have several pieces of equipment to bring in and get set up. With this many people in the room, this would be very difficult to do, so we will have to ask you to be kind enough to leave the room.

Here is what we will ask you to do for this ten-minute period of waiting. We have on this floor a number of additional rooms, so that each of you, if you would like, can wait alone in your own room. These rooms are comfortable and spacious; they all have armchairs, and there are books and magazines in each room. It did occur to us, however, that some of you might want to wait for these ten minutes together with some of the other girls here. If you would prefer this, of course, just let us know. We'll take one of the empty classrooms on this floor and you can wait together with some of the other girls there.

The experimenter then passed out a sheet on which the subjects could indicate their preference. This sheet read as follows:

Please indicate below whether you prefer waiting your turn to be shocked alone or in the company of others.

———I prefer being alone.
———I prefer being with others.
———I really don't care.

In order to get a measure of the intensity of the subjects' desires to be alone or together, the experimenter continued:

With a group this size and with the number of additional rooms we have, it's not always possible to give each girl exactly what she'd like. So be perfectly honest and let us know how much you'd like to be alone or together with other girls. Let us know just how you feel, and we'll use that information to come as close as possible to putting you into the arrangement of your choice.

The experimenter then passed out the following scale:

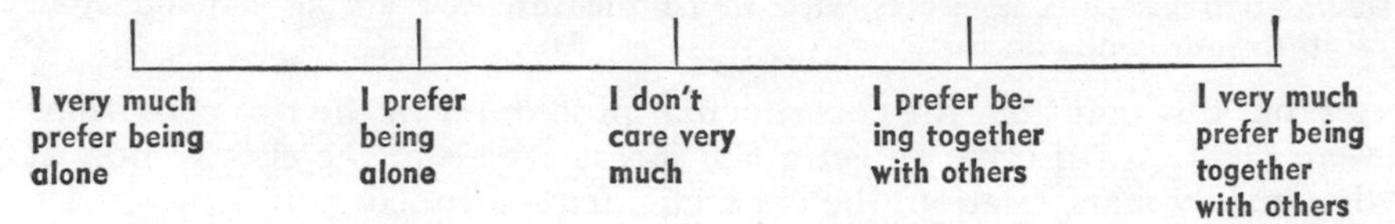

To get a final measure of the effectiveness of the anxiety manipulation, the experimenter continued:

It has, of course, occurred to us that some of you may not wish to take part in this experiment. Now, we would find it perfectly understandable if some of you should feel that you do not want to be a subject in an experiment in which you will be shocked. If this is the case just let us know. I'll pass out this sheet on which you may indicate whether or not you want to go on. If you do wish to be a subject, check "yes"; if you do not wish to take part, check "no" and you may leave. Of course, if you check "no" we cannot give you credit in your psychology classes for having taken part in this experiment.

After the subjects had marked their sheets, the experiment was over and the experimenter took off his white coat and explained in detail the purpose of the experiment and the reasons for the various deceptions practiced. The cooperation of the subjects was of course enlisted in not talking about the experiment to other students.

In summary, in this experimental set-up, anxiety has been manipulated by varying the fear of being shocked. The affiliative tendency is measured by the subject's preference for "Alone," "Together," or "Don't care" and by the expressed intensity of this preference.

SUBJECTS

The subjects in this study were all young women, students in Introductory Psychology courses at the University of Minnesota. At the beginning of each semester, students in these classes may sign up for a subject pool. More than 90 percent of the students usually do so, for they receive one additional point on their final examination for each experimental hour they serve. This fact should be kept in mind when considering the proportion of subjects who refused to continue in the experiment. The experimental sessions were run with groups of five to eight women at a time, for a total of 32 subjects in the high-anxiety condition and 30 subjects in the low-anxiety condition.

RESULTS

Table 1 presents data permitting evaluation of the effectiveness of the manipulation of anxiety. The column labeled "Anxiety" presents the mean score, by condition, of responses to the question "How do you feel about being shocked?" The greater the score, the greater the anxiety;

a score greater than 3 indicates dislike. Clearly there are large and significant differences between the two conditions.

TABLE 1
EFFECTIVENESS OF THE ANXIETY MANIPULATION

	Number of Subjects	*Anxiety*	*% of Subjects Refusing to Continue*
High Anxiety	32	3.69	18.8
Low Anxiety	30	2.48	0

The results of the second measure of anxiety, a subject's willingness to continue in the experiment when given the opportunity to drop out, are presented in the column labeled "% of subjects refusing to continue." This is, perhaps, the best single indicator of the effectiveness of the manipulation, for it is a reality-bound measure. Again it is clear that the manipulation of anxiety has been successful. Some 19 percent of subjects in the high-anxiety condition refused to continue in the experiment. All subjects in the low-anxiety condition were willing to go through with the experiment.

The effect of anxiety on the affiliative tendency may be noted in Table 2, where, for each condition, the number of subjects choosing "Together," "Alone," or "Don't Care" is tabulated. It is evident that there is a strong positive relationship between anxiety and the index of affiliative tendency, the proportion of subjects choosing the "Together" alternative. Some 63 percent of subjects in the high-anxiety condition wanted to be together with other subjects while they waited to be shocked. In the low-anxiety condition only 33 percent of the subjects wished to be together.

TABLE 2
RELATIONSHIP OF ANXIETY TO THE AFFILIATIVE TENDENCY

	Number Choosing			*Overall Intensity*
	Together	*Don't Care*	*Alone*	
High Anxiety	20	9	3	+.88
Low Anxiety	10	18	2	+.35

The column labeled "Overall Intensity" in Table 2 presents the mean score for all subjects, in each condition, of responses to the scale designed to measure the intensity of the desire to be alone or together with others. The point "I don't care very much" is scored as zero. The two points on this scale indicating a preference for being together with other subjects are scored as +1 and +2 respectively. The points indicating a preference for being alone are scored as −1 and −2. The mean scores of this scale provide the best overall index of the magnitude of affiliative desires, for this score combines choice and intensity of choice. Also, this index incorporates the relatively milder preferences of subjects who chose the "Don't Care" alternative, for 30 percent of these subjects did express some preference on this scale. Again it is clear that affiliative desires increase with anxiety. The mean intensity score for high-anxiety subjects is +.88 and for low-anxiety subjects is +.35.

Expectations, then, are confirmed, but confirmed, in truth, in a blaze of ambiguity, for the several terms of the formulation "anxiety leads to the arousal of affiliative tendencies" are still vague. What is meant by the "affiliative tendency," and precisely why do the subjects choose to be together when anxious? What is meant by "anxiety," and what are the limits of this relationship? What is meant by "leads to," and, historically, just how and why is this relationship established?

* * *

A series of studies addressed to these questions are reported by Stanley Schachter in *The Psychology of Affiliation* (Stanford, Calif.: Stanford University Press, 1959).

The Provisions of Social Relationships

Robert S. Weiss

The problem of what we gain through relationships with others has been central in the study of human experience. A number of theoretical responses to this problem are explicit or seem to be implicit in current work. It may be of value to review two of these, since in combination they served as initial orientation for the investigations reported here.[1]

The first theory proposes that individuals possess a "fund of sociability," a readiness and need to interact with others, which may be distributed in various ways, but is in any event of constant amount.[2] In this

This paper was prepared especially for this volume. An earlier version was read at a conference of the Harvard Program on Technology and Science in 1967 and subsequently published as "Materials for a theory of social relationships," in Warren G. Bennis, et al. (eds.), *Interpersonal Dynamics*, 2nd edition (Homewood, Illinois: Dorsey, 1968), pp. 154–163. The work reported in this paper has been supported by grants from NIMH, including a Research Scientist Development Award, 5 KO2 MH45731.

1 Other theoretical orientations, distinct from those discussed here, include: the treatment of all relationships as simply opportunities for exchange; the view that relationships are imposed on individuals by the social structure; instinct theories which see relationships as channels for expression of individual propensities; the division of relationships into those which are security-seeking and those which are satisfaction-seeking, which occurs in the work of both Karen Horney and Harry Stack Sullivan; the views of Freud, in which relationships appear to be resultants of the expression of the individual's binding energies; and the views of the various "object relations" schools of psychoanalysis, in which relationships may be established for common-sense reasons, but almost invariably become freighted with infantile concerns regarding security and satisfaction. These rapid characterizations of necessity give no indication of the richness of observation and thought present in the writings of representatives of each point of view. They may suggest, however, the range of approaches to the problem of the functions of social ties.

2 The fund of sociability idea has been put forward by Joel I. Nelson in "Clique contacts and family orientations," *American Sociological Review,* Vol. 31, No. 5 (October, 1966), pp. 663–672. He points out that a similar statement is contained in the work of Elizabeth Bott, *Family and Social Network* (London: Tavistock, 1957).

view individuals might with equal satisfaction engage in a great deal of intense contact with a few others, or in a more limited amount of less intense contact with a great many others. They would encounter difficulty only if the demands on the fund were too great or the opportunities for expenditure from the fund too limited or, possibly, if the channels available for expenditure were for some reason uncongenial.

The second theory is that of the "mediating primary group." This theory distinguishes between the provisions of "primary relationships," which are close, frequent, face-to-face, and accompanied by warmth and commitment, and the provisions of "secondary relationships" which are for the most part instrumental, perhaps necessary for the achievement of an occupational or economic aim, but in any event of little emotional importance. Examples of primary relationships would include relationships with one's family and close friends; examples of secondary relationships would include relationships required by work, relationships with fellow members of formal organizations, and emotionally unimportant relationships with acquaintances and with individuals who provide services. The theory proposes that our beliefs, attitudes, and understandings were formed in primary groups to which we once belonged and are now maintained in good part through interaction with other members of primary groups to which we currently belong. It holds that without any primary group affiliation we would drift into a state of normlessness or anomie. It also holds that our morale, our sense of well-being, is sustained by membership in primary groups, and that without any primary group affiliations we would become despairing. Withdrawal from primary contacts would be seen as dangerous to an individual's cognitive and emotional states, whereas an individual might withdraw from secondary contacts and yet not find himself in difficulty so long as he continued to be an active participant in one or more primary groups.[3]

The first empirical materials I want to present come from a study of the Parents Without Partners organization.[4] This is a national association of fairly autonomous local chapters, each providing a variety of programs for parents who are for any reason alone. For about a year a colleague

---

The theory was considered but rejected by Theodore Caplow and Robert Forman in their "Neighborhood interactions in a homogeneous community," *American Sociological Review,* Vol. 15, No. 2 (June, 1950), pp. 357–366. A theory which, though not identical, resembles fund-of-sociability is contained in Philip Slater's "On social regression," *American Sociological Review,* Vol. 28, No. 3 (June, 1963), pp. 339–364. This paper discusses alternative deployments of what is assumed to be a constant amount of libidinal energy.

[3] The ideas referred to here have a long history in both German and American sociology. A valuable review is given by Edward Shils in "The study of the primary group," Daniel Lerner and Harold Lasswell (eds.), *The Policy Sciences* (Stanford, California: Stanford University Press, 1951), pp. 44–69.

[4] See, for a report of this study, "The contributions of an organization of single parents to the well-being of its members," *Family Coordinator* (July, 1973), pp. 321–326.

and I attended meetings of the Boston chapter, participated in programs, and interviewed current and former members. Two research questions concerned us: first, what loss had these individuals sustained with the dissolution of their marriage; and second, in what way did membership compensate for the loss? Our initial hypothesis, on beginning the study, was based on an underlying view which combined elements of the two theories just described. We assumed that individuals require a certain amount of "primary" contact—which we interpreted as contact in which emotions might be expressed—and this amount might be obtained either through a great deal of interaction within a single relationship or through less intense interaction within a number of relationships.

We found that although Parents Without Partners offered single parents assistance with a host of difficulties they were likely to encounter in their social life and in their roles as parents, most members seemed indeed to have joined simply because they were lonely. Their loneliness seemed to have been a direct consequencc of their loss of the marital relationship, rather than a secondary consequence of the change in their social roles or the increase in financial strain which might have accompanied the dissolution of their marriage. A qualification to the observation that most members of the organization had joined because they were lonely might be that this seemed to have been less true when the marriage had not been the only source of emotional interchange in the member's life; an example would be a woman who had been extremely close, before the dissolution of her marriage, to her mother, to a sister, or to a girl friend.[5]

Our assumption regarding the need of individuals for a certain amount of primary contact led us to expect that members of Parents Without Partners would report that their initial loneliness had been reduced after participation in the organization. We anticipated that members would report that friendly interaction with other members had in some degree compensated for their loss. We found, however, that although many members, particularly among the women, specifically mentioned friendship as a major contribution of the organization to their well-being, and although these friendships often became very close and very important to the participants, they did not especially diminish their loneliness. They made the loneliness easier to manage, by providing reassurance that it was not the individual's fault, but rather was common to all those in the individual's situation.[6] And they provided the support of friends

[5] The family literature contains a number of descriptions of marriages in which both husband and wife maintain close relationships with same-sex peers or in which the wife remains close to her mother despite her marriage. See, for example, Mirra Komarovsky, *Blue-Collar Marriage* (New York: Random House, 1962).

[6] For both men and women loneliness could be allayed by the formation of a new committed cross-sex relationship. Further materials on this topic can be found in Robert S. Weiss, *Loneliness* (Cambridge, Massachusetts: M.I.T. Press, 1974).

who could understand because they were dealing with the same difficulties. One woman described the benefits and limitations of friendship in these words: "Sometimes I have the girls over, and we talk about how hard it is. Misery loves company, you know."

At this point it was clear that friendships, however valuable they are in other respects, do not supply the loneliness-allaying provision that is supplied by marriage. This raised the question of whether friendship was too weak a relationship to supply this loneliness-allaying provision adequately, or whether friendship was organized to provide something quite different, perhaps something that might not be found in marriage. To decide between these alternatives we needed to find people who were married, but without friends. If marriage and friendship made different provisions, then we should find that individuals without friends experienced distress, even though they were married. If on the other hand marriage made the same provisions as friendship, but more intensely, we should find these individuals to get along almost as well as married people who did have friends.

We began with a pilot study of six couples who had moved to the Boston suburbs from at least two states away. We have since extended this work, with corroboration of our initial findings, and our initial findings have also been corroborated by others.[7]

We found in four of our initial newcomer couples that after a period of time without friends the wife experienced severe distress, different in quality, but comparable in intensity, to the loneliness that followed the dissolution of a marriage. Despite the warmth which might exist in her marriage, the woman was likely to become painfully bored, to develop a sense of marginality, to feel that her day was without structure and her activities without meaning. She might pine for social activity, just as those who had lost their marriage might pine for someone to be close to.

This condition was sometimes also described by the term "loneliness," despite its difference from the "loneliness" reported by members of Parents Without Partners. To distinguish between the two conditions, we referred to the former as "the loneliness of social isolation," and to the latter as "the loneliness of emotional isolation."

In the remaining two newcomer couples the wife seemed to have escaped the loneliness of social isolation, but the means of her escape was instructive. In one the husband had chosen to move into a new development where many of the other families were also newcomers. He then invited other couples to his home and in this way brought his wife in contact with other women with whom she could establish a social network. In the second couple, one in which there were no children, the wife

[7] See *Loneliness, op. cit.,* and the study by Myrna M. Weissman and Eugene S. Paykel reported therein.

escaped social isolation by entering the work world herself. Yet this solution did not seem entirely happy; the husband and wife appeared both to be so engaged by striving to achieve acceptance at work that their marriage was emotionally empty.

For the women who stayed at home the relationship with the husband could to an extent ameliorate the loneliness of social isolation, but it could not entirely dissipate it. Husbands could not really discuss with interest the dilemmas of child care nor the burdens of housework, and though they sometimes tried, they simply could not function properly as a friend. Moreover, what the women needed was not so much a single friend as access to a social network, to a community of friends, who might together exchange information about matters of common interest, establish values, and create social events and activities.

The husbands themselves had such a social network on their jobs. But while this network provided them with adequate social integration, it left undecided for the time being its assessment of their worth. As newcomers to the work situation, the men had yet to prove themselves. And so the husbands were dealing with quite different issues from those engaging their wives, issues that often were equally productive of tension. Because in these couples the husband's problems were different from the wife's, neither could entirely understand what was happening to the other.

On the basis of our work with newcomers it appeared to us that in the absence of membership in a social network which shared their central life concerns, individuals experience severe distress. Just as the provisions of marriage cannot be supplied by friendships, so too the provisions of friendships cannot be supplied by marriage.

These findings are incompatible with the fund of sociability idea that relationships are relatively undifferentiated in their provisions. They are also incompatible with the idea that the essential distinction among relationships is between those which are primary and those which are secondary. Both marriage and friendship are close and face-to-face, yet their provisions are distinct. We are led to form another hypothesis regarding the nature of relational provisions. This is the hypothesis that different types of relationships make different provisions, all of which may be required by individuals, at least under some conditions.

With this hypothesis in mind we returned to Parents Without Partners and tried to catalogue the different relationships individuals formed with one another within the organization, or reported having established outside the organization. We also attempted to identify the provisions of each of these relationships.

While so doing, we assimilated to our developing theoretical framework some further suppositions regarding the nature of relationships. These begin with the supposition that individuals have requirements for well-being which can only be met within relationships. It is only within relationships, for example, that one can exchange information and observations regarding matters of common interest, or feel the loyalty and support of another, or take responsibility for another's well-being.

It seems likely that individuals maintain relationships in order to gain their provisions. Different relational provisions, however, would depend on different and ordinarily incompatible relational assumptions. The assumptions that underlie a friendship, for example, and that make possible the free exchange of observations between the friends, are different, and incompatible with, the assumptions that underlie relationships with children.

Because one set of underlying assumptions is required for one sort of provision and another set for another sort of provision, relationships tend to become specialized in their provisions. As a result individuals must maintain a number of different relationships to establish the conditions necessary for well-being.

The specialization of relationships is probably always incomplete. Undoubtedly there is a certain amount of nurturance even in friendship, although one would imagine ordinarily not a great deal, and in a similar fashion some slight element of almost every relational provision in every relationship. There may be times when participants in a particular relationship have great need for provisions different from those the relationship ordinarily makes, and the normal assumptions of the relationship are temporarily flooded out; for example, participants in a friendship may respond to a sudden need for intimate exchange. One consequence of such temporary redefinition may be uneasiness between the individuals when they attempt to reinstate the former assumptions of the relationship.

Although there are many variations in the way people organize their lives, there are reliable associations between types of relationships and their provisions. One can in general say that relations with kin seem to be based on a sense of alliance and provide sources of help if needed; that friendships offer provisions associated with community of interest; that marital relationships make a number of provisions, including a sense of reliable attachment. The marital relationship may be an exception to the generalization that relationships specialize in their provisions. Indeed, marriages seem to be based on the assumption that whatever either participant needs should be available within the relationship. But the consequence for marriages can be disappointment and frustration when the assumptions necessary for one provision conflict with those necessary for another; when, for example, the functioning of the marriage as a partnership impedes its functioning as a source of support or as a source of companionship. The non-specialization of provisions within marriage may stem from the attachment provision of marriage. I cannot take the space here to pursue this issue, but there is reason to suspect that attachment relationships, partly because they sponsor continuing proximity, tend toward multiplicity of provision.

On the basis of our work we believe we can identify six categories of relational provisions, each ordinarily associated with a particular type of relationship. Each of these provisions requires a relationship whose assumptions are different from those of other relationships, and we would therefore expect that relationships that provide each would tend to be specialized, with the possible exception of attachment-providing relationships.

1. *Attachment* is provided by relationships from which participants gain a sense of security and place. In the presence of attachment-providing relationships individuals feel comfortable and at home. In the absence of relationships providing attachment individuals feel lonely and restless. Attachment is provided by marriage, by other cross-sex committed relationships; among some women by relationships with a close friend, a sister, or mother; among some men by relationships with "buddies." [8]

2. *Social integration* is provided by relationships in which participants share concerns, or even better, by a network of such relationships. Membership in a network of common-concern relationships permits the development of pooled information and ideas and a shared interpretation of experience. It provides, in addition, a source of companionship and opportunities for exchange of services, especially in the area of common interest. The network offers a base for social events and happenings, for social engagement and social activity. In the absence of such relationships life becomes dull, perhaps painfully so.[9]

3. *Opportunity for nurturance* is provided by relationships in which the adult takes responsibility for the well-being of a child and so can develop a sense of being needed. Responsibility for children seems to provide meaning to an individual's life and to sustain commitment to goals in a wide variety of activities. Individuals without children, on encountering serious reverse, may be tempted to "let themselves go." In

[8] For a discussion of the provision of attachment by marriage see Robert O. Blood, Jr., and Donald Wolfe, *Husbands and Wives* (Free Press, 1960), particularly their chapter seven, "Understanding and emotional well-being." This issue is discussed also by the forthcoming books, Robert S. Weiss, *Marital Separation* (New York: Basic Books), and Ira O. Glick, Robert S. Weiss, and C. Murray Parkes, *The First Year of Bereavement* (New York: Wiley-Interscience). For one instance of attachment in another relationship see "Buddy relations and combat performance," by Roger Little, *The New Military*, edited by Morris Janowitz (Russell Sage, 1964).

[9] Studies of retired men suggest that they sometimes experience boredom and restlessness similar to the condition we found among newcomer wives. See Eugene A. Friedmann and Robert J. Havighurst, *The Meaning of Work and Retirement* (Chicago, 1954). For evidence that friendships between middle-class couples are better characterized as "common interest relationships," than as "attachment," though they contain genuine elements of loyalty and affection, see Nicholas Babchuk and Alan P. Bates, "The primary relations of middle-class couples: a study in male dominance," *American Sociological Review* (June, 1963), pp. 377–384.

contrast, individuals with children have reported that the children gave them reason for going on living.[10]

4. *Reassurance of worth* is provided by relationships which attest to an individual's competence in a social role. Colleague relationships function in this way for some men, particularly for men whose work is difficult or highly valued. Relationships within the family may function in this way for other men for whom a sense of competence depends not on particular skills, but rather on their ability to support the family. For women who work, just as for men, reassurance of worth may be provided by relationships with colleagues. For women who stay home, relationships with husbands, children, and acquaintances who recognize their home-making skills, may make this provision.[11]

5. *A sense of reliable alliance* is provided primarily by kin. Only within kin ties, especially those between siblings or lineal kin, can one expect continuing assistance whether there is a mutual affection or not, whether one has reciprocated for past help or not. We would surmise that individuals cut off from their families, or without familial relationships, would feel constantly limited to their own resources and at times vulnerable and abandoned.[12]

6. *The obtaining of guidance* seems to be important to individuals when they are in stressful situations. At such times it seems important for individuals to have access to a relationship with an apparently trustworthy and authoritative figure who can furnish them with emotional support and assist them in formulating and sustaining a line of action.[13]

I would conjecture that an adequate life organization is one that makes available a set of relationships that, together, can furnish all the above relational provisions. Not all these provisions will be of equal importance for all individuals. Different phases in life, different immediate concerns, and perhaps different character structures and different tastes may make

[10] These observations are further developed in *Marital Separation, op. cit.*, and *The First Year of Bereavement, op. cit.*

[11] In at least one discussion virtually all motivations for work are reduced to a need for "ego-recognition"; see Rensis Likert, *New Patterns of Management* (New York: McGraw-Hill: 1961). See also, for data regarding the analogous valuings of housework, Robert S. Weiss and Nancy M. Samuelson, "Feelings of worth among American women, *Marriage and Family Living* (Nov., 1957).

[12] The importance of help in the relationships of parents and grown children is attested to by, among others, Marvin Sussman, "The help pattern in the middle-class family," *American Sociological Review, 18* (Feb., 1953), pp. 22–28. See also, for the subjective experience of being separated from kin on a holiday devoted to the celebration of kin ties, "Christmas in an apartment-hotel," Mark Benney, Robert S. Weiss, Rolf Meyersohn and David Riesman, *American Journal of Sociology* (Nov., 1959) *65,* pp. 233–240.

[13] For observations regarding the functioning of such relationships, and the difficulty individuals without resources may have in obtaining them, see Robert S. Weiss, "Helping relationships: relationships with physicians, social workers, priests, and others," *Social Problems, 20* (Winter, 1973), pp. 319–328.

for different valuings among the relational provisions. But one would assume that an adequate life organization would make possible the gaining of each provision as it is felt necessary.

Attachment relationships require a sense of nearly steady accessibility. The relationship that provides attachment may in consequence be of central importance in the establishment of a life organization; we might think of individuals organizing their lives around whatever relationship provides them with attachment. For most individuals this will be marriage or some other form of reliable cross-sex relationship. For some it may be a relationship with a grown child or with an intimate friend. Other relationships would then be integrated with this central relationship. Since other relational provisions can, like attachment, be supplied by a variety of relationships, quite different life organizations may potentially make available all needed relational provisions. Of course different life patterns will have different implications for individual flexibility, growth, stability, or immunity from risk of loss or relational deficit. Some patterns of life organization may in general work out better than others or be more to a particular individual's liking than others. But with these qualifications, it would appear that a variety of life organizations can potentially make available the relational provisions an individual might require.

I would conjecture that the absence of a required relational provision would be signalled by distress, and, moreover, that the form of the distress would be specific to the provision which was in deficit. I have already noted that the absence of attachment results in the loneliness of emotional isolation, and the absence of social integration in the loneliness of social isolation. I would also propose that the absence of opportunity for nurturance would on occasion give rise to a sense of meaninglessness, the absence of support for a sense of worth to low self-regard, the absence of a secure alliance to a sense of vulnerability, and the absence of a guidance-providing relationship, should the individual be under severe stress, to uncertainty and anxiety. It is difficult to say that some deficits give rise to more severe distress than others; that absence of attachment, for example, is more disorganizing than absence of opportunity for nurturance. One can cite childless couples who are as downcast by difficulty in arranging for an adoption as any lonely person might be by difficulty in finding love. Any deficit seems to create a condition of restless distress.

What I have sketched here is only a framework for thinking about relationships, lightly filled in with observations and conjecture. Any number of questions remain to be answered: what are the different needs of individuals in different phases of life, whose personalities are different, who differ from one another in life conditions and in aims? What are the different ways individuals can establish reliable attachments, and all the rest? And what are the advantages and disadvantages of different life organizations? What are the social and emotional consequences of the loss of particular relational provisions, and what are the social and emotional implications of a life which is for a long period of time defective in that it is without some one or more relational provisions?

These are, of course, questions we puzzle over throughout our own lives. My hope is that it is possible to pursue their study systematically.

"Getting It All Together": Some Group Issues in Communes

Rosabeth Moss Kanter

Communes are both an old and a new social form. Some kind of communal living was practiced by a small number of groups in the United States even before its establishment as a nation, and many groups today look to those older traditons for their inspiration. On the other hand, today's communes are new in their large numbers, high visibility, and limited goals. While many communal groups of the past were a response to institutional strains in the society (religious, economic, or political), and sought to become full-fledged alternative communities, today's communes are more often a response to interpersonal and psychological strains in the society, and want to become a new kind of family. Many communes today seek to recreate a romanticized version of the extended family, in a search for intense, intimate, participatory, meaningful, group-based ways of life. In the midst of an advanced technological society seen as insulating, meaningless, fragmented, and machine-like, today's utopians seek a shared life. They desire freedom and the concomitant ability to define their own life conditions. They want to be "together" in all ways that the new counter-culture uses this word: inner peace and self-acceptance; whole person relating to whole person; barriers of ego, property, sex, age disappearing.

The result of today's quest for togetherness is the vast number of experiments in communal living springing up across the country. There are small urban groups sharing living quarters and raising their families together while holding outside jobs. There are rural farming communes combining work life and family life under one roof. There are formal organizations with their own business enterprises, like the Bruderhof communities, which manufacture Community Playthings; and there are loose aggregates of people without even a name for their group.

Abridged from the *American Journal of Orthopsychiatry*, 1972, *42*, 632–643, with permission of the author and the American Orthopsychiatric Association.

The extent of the commune movement is vast, but similarly vast are the problems of building viable communities. Today's communal movement represents a reawakening of the search for utopia that has been carried out in America from as early as 1680, when the first religious sects retreated to the wilderness to live in community. But while experiments in communal living have always been part of the American landscape, only a few dozen of these ventures survived for more than a few years. Building community has proven to be difficult, and today's communes fall heir to the difficulties.

COMMUNES OF THE PAST

Previous research[1] has uncovered some of the things that distinguished successful communes of the past. In order to learn about the kinds of things that make a commune work, this research compared thirty nineteenth-century American communes—nine that lasted thirty-three years or more (called "successful") with twenty-one that existed less than sixteen years and on the average about four years ("unsuccessful"). Among the communes in the study were the Shakers, Oneida, Amana, Harmony, New Harmony, and Brook Farm. The study asked over 120 questions about the presence or absence of certain social arrangements that build commitment and create a strong group.

Successful nineteenth-century communities built strong commitment to their group through the kinds of sacrifices and investments members made for and in the community, through discouraging extra-group ties and building strong family feeling within the community, through identity change processes for members, and through ideological systems and authority structures that gave meaning and direction to the community.

Long-lived communities tended to require some sacrifices of their members as a test of faith, and full investment of money and property, so that participants had a stake in the fate of the community. They tended to ensure the concentration of loyalty within the community by geographical separation and by discouraging contact with the outside. They spread affection throughout the whole community by discouraging exclusive relationships based on two-person attraction or biological family—through either free love (in which sexual contact with all others was required) or celibacy (in which no one had sexual contact) and separation of biological families with communal child-rearing. These mechanisms aimed at creating an equal share in man-woman and adult-child relationships for everyone. Family feeling was enhanced by selection of a homogeneous

[1] R. Kanter, *Commitment and Community: Utopias and Communes in Sociological Perspective* (Cambridge, Mass.: Harvard University Press, 1972); also R. Kanter, "Commitment and social organization: a study of commitment mechanisms in utopian communities," *Amer. Soc. Rev.* 33 (Aug. 1968), 499–517.

group of members; by full communistic sharing of property; by communistic labor in which no jobs were compensated, everyone shared equally in community benefits, jobs were rotated through the membership, and some work was done by the whole community; by regular group contact through meetings (routine decision-making ones and T-group-like sessions); and by rituals emphasizing the communion of the whole. Identity change processes in long-lived communes tended to consist of T-group-like mutual criticism sessions in which issues of commitment and deviance and meeting of community standards were examined, and through stratification systems that accorded deference to those best living up to community norms. Long-lived communes tended to have elaborate ideologies providing purpose and meaning for community life and an ultimate guide and justification for decisions. There tended to be strong central figures, charismatic leaders who symbolized the community's values and who made final decisions for the community and set structural guidelines. Finally, they tended to require ideological conversion for admissions and did not automatically admit all applicants.

What was found, then, was that successful nineteenth-century utopias developed a number of ways of dealing with group relations, property, work, values, and leadership—all of which created an enduring commitment, involving motivation to work, will to continue, fellowship, and cohesion as a group. At the same time that this enabled the successful communities to survive in terms of longevity, such practices also created strong communities in the utopian sense and fulfilled many of the desires impelling people toward community today. The successful groups provided for their members strong feelings of participation, involvement, and belonging to a family group. They built a world centered around sharing—of property, of work, of living space, of feelings, of values. They offered identity and meaning, a value-oriented life of direction and purpose.

TODAY'S COMMUNES

Today's communes[2] are different from those of the past, however, in that the vast majority of them tend to be small in size, anarchic in philosophy, and seeking family-style intimacy without much else in the way of a utopian platform. There *are* a number that resemble the successful communes of the past—Synanon, the Bruderhof communities on the East Coast, some religiously-oriented groups, a few older, more established communes. But most of the new communes range in size from six to forty people and reject the rigid structuring of group life true of past

[2] Material on contemporary communes comes from a questionnaire study, field visits and observation of several dozen groups, secondary sources, and personal experience in a commune.

communes. "Do your own thing" is a pervasive ethic. Yet, despite this ethic, and despite variations in style or ideological orientation, all communes of any size or length of existence share one important issue: creating a group out of a diverse collection of individuals.

The kind of group today's communes wish to build is one that provides the warmth and intimacy of a family. A hippie commune of 50 people in California, for example, called itself "the Lynch family," and all members adopted the last name of the founder. A New Mexico commune at one time called itself The Chosen Family; a New York City group, simply "the family." The Fort Hill community in Roxbury, Massachusetts, reports that it has evolved a family structure, with all members brothers and sisters, and the leader, Mel Lyman, the father at the head of the family.

For some communes, becoming a family means collective child-rearing: shared responsibility for raising children. Children as well as adults, for example, in a Vermont commune, have their own separate rooms, and they consider all the adults in the community their "parents." Other communes are interested in sexual experimentation, in changing the man-woman relationship from monogamy, an exclusive two-person bond, to group marriage, in which many attachments throughout the community are possible and encouraged.

Behind these practices lies the desire to create intense involvement with the communal group as a whole—feelings of connectedness and belonging and the warmth of many attachments.

CREATING A GROUP

While communes seek to become families, they are, at the same time, something different from families; they are groups with their own unique form, something between communities, organizations, families, and friendship groups, and they may contain families in their midst.

Each commune must create its own social form from scratch; it must cope afresh with those group issues that are at least partially pre-solved for families or other accepted institutions in our society. Part of the definition of a commune, in fact, is that it is a group that comes together to create for itself its own form.

Communes, like other groups, start with certain goals or ideas, sometimes well-defined, sometimes vague. Their social structure comes about through the process of coping with several important group issues, in the context of their ideals. These issues revolve around how the commune becomes a group and comes to define itself with respect to its environment.

Even the most organized nineteenth- and twentieth-century communes did not spring into being full-blown from a blueprint. Instead, they went through periods of anarchy, chaos, non-direction, high turnover, and open boundaries as they struggled to translate global ideals about community into specific behavior. The development of social organization is a step-wise process, and the history of many communes demonstrates this. The Bruderhof are now over fifty years old and well-organized. But in its early years in Germany, the community struggled with issues of developing a group identity and defining the group's boundaries. In fact, during its first summer, the now-traditional, straight-laced, and organized religious group resembled many of today's new communes. It began with no financial resources, an open-door policy (that brought floods of strange characters and curiosity seekers), and no clear notion of how to translate ideology into practice. The numbers of people grew and declined (more in summer, fewer in winter), living conditions were primitive, and the vast majority of members came from urban backgrounds and knew nothing of farming. They rented rather than owned their quarters. But group cohesion was promoted through song and celebration of all events, from picking up stones to hoeing beans. And out of the interaction of the diverse people who came together, group coherence gradually developed. The first crisis dealt with how the group would support itself, finding a task in which cooperation and shared fate would be embodied. Ideological and practical disagreements led to the definition of boundaries: who could become a member and who could not; which characteristics of members would be supported, which changed; what the focus of the group was to be.[3]

Similarly, some of Israel's kibbutzim in their early years also strongly resembled the budding period of today's youth communes. The kibbutz studied by Spiro[4] grew out of the German youth movement. A number of urban young people migrated to Palestine together, partly out of shared rebellion against their parents and urban life and partly out of a sense of adventure. When they actually found themselves in Palestine, they had little idea of what to do next. An intense, profound emotional experience provided the bond that translated itself gradually into the development of communal institutions. Other kibbutz researchers have indicated that early kibbutzim, like many American hippie communes, went through periods of anarchism and unwillingness to organize or set limits, before growing into the strong communities of today.

The same step-wise development of organization can be seen in the history of American communes of the past. Oneida started as an informal Bible discussion group in Putney, Vermont. Personnel changed, ideas and institutions developed, ideologies grew to explain and justify the practices that members found they preferred. As a group, they finally moved

[3] E. Arnold, *Torches Together: The Beginnings and Early Years of the Bruderhof Communities* (Rifton, N.Y.: Plough Publishing, 1964).

[4] M. Spiro, *Kibbutz: Venture in Utopia* (Cambridge, Mass.: Harvard University Press, 1956).

to Oneida, New York, several years later, and created a full-scale, well-organized, long-lasting communal village.

The ideologies and social practices of communes, then, can be seen as more than an outgrowth of utopian values. They are the solutions arrived at in face-to-face interactions and daily life to the crucial issue all new and non-institutionalized social groups face: how to become a group.

GROUP ISSUES

The first important issue is admission to the group: how does a person become a member? There are societally-delimited ways of entering a family—through marriage, birth, or legal adoption—but no similar guidelines for joining a commune. In American society, strangers do not knock at the doors of residences, asking to become a member of the family, but they *do* approach communes with this request. Many modern communes began with the wish to be open to all comers, and some still operate on the "open land" concept; anyone can come and stake out a bit of territory on the property. In strong contrast to the successful communities of the past, which required an ideological commitment for membership or had some screening procedure, some modern communes do not even make a member/nonmember distinction; whoever is there at the time "belongs." But as the group begins to define itself, it also begins to define criteria and procedures for membership, an issue that many communes are reluctant to face. Some limit membership by the size of their property, others ask that people come in for probationary periods first; gradually, even some of the more anarchic communes are beginning to control entry. The consequences of failing to control it are sometimes demoralizing for the group, as a resident of Morningstar Ranch said in 1967 about its leader's open admission policy:

> It's not like it used to be. Too many outsiders have been coming up here during the summer—Hell's Angels, tourists, people who come up for the wrong reasons. I don't know if [he's] right, letting everybody in.[5]

By contrast, the viable communes of the past all had selective entry procedures.

"Getting it all together" is a central group issue—to find sources of cohesion, to create and solidify the bonds holding the group together. In communes, several things may happen to provide sources of cohesion. One is the development of belief in the group's superiority. Nineteenth-century communities had elaborate beliefs of this kind, certain that they were heralding a new age, bringing about the millenium, and that, by

[5] K. Lamott, "Doing Their Own Thing at Morningstar," *Horizon* 10 (Spring 1968), 14–19.

contrast, the surrounding society was sinful. The Oneida community felt that contact with the outside was sufficiently contaminating that after visitors left, the whole community joined to clean the buildings in a ritualistic purification. What a sense of membership in their own special group the Oneidans must have had—to scrub away traces of contact with non-Oneidans. The Shakers developed to a high art their condemnation of non-Shakers and of the previous non-Shaker life of Shaker converts. One example is a hymn in which Shakers indicated their great love for other Shakers after first expressing their deep hatred for their biological families:

> Of all the relations that ever I see
> My old fleshly kindred are furthest from me
> O how ugly they look, how hateful they feel
> To see them and hate them increases my zeal.

We can see parallels to the Shakers today in the bitterness with which some communards condemn their parents or, more often, the life that their parents have led. Thc firm rejection of other ways of life, particularly those representing options once open to commune members, helps reinforce the belief that the commune is, indeed, a special, valuable, worthwhile place. What parents also represent is a set of ties that not all members of the commune share—yet the cohesiveness of the group is dependent in part on elevating that which is shared to a higher moral and emotional place than that which cannot be included in the group or shared by all members. "What we have together is more beautiful than what we have apart" is echoed by many communes. Also recurrent is: "What we have and are *now* is more important and worthwhile than what we may have been separately." In some communes this results in a noticeable lack of interest in members' pasts, and even resentment at talking much about life before the group—in T-group language, the "there and then" rather than the "here and now."

A researcher[6] at a communal farm in Oregon reports that the ten adults there knew relatively little about each other's backgrounds. ("We accept a person for what he is, not what he was.") A woman living with her husband in an urban commune reported to me the awkwardness and uneasiness she experienced when her parents came to visit her in the commune. They were a reminder of her non-communal past, as well as being people with whom she shared something that other commune members could not share.

Belief in the group's specialness is one step away from belief in its superiority, and a big theme in the commune culture is superiority of their way of life over others. One rural commune prides itself on the purity and naturalness of its existence, as opposed to the corruption of the city. A member said, "In the city you don't even know your own *motives*."

[6] R. Harmer, *Bedrock* (mimeo), Harvard Business School, Boston.

Many of these sources of solidarity are dependent on the existence of a wider society—the group becomes special by specifying who and what it is not, who and what it rejects. But, at the same time, communes struggle with defining what they *are*. At this point the issue of common purpose becomes essential: what are we trying to make happen together? What goal or idea or symbol "gets it all together"? This is a major problem for many modern communes, particularly anarchistically-oriented ones. They tend to come together in the shared rejection of the established society, particularly of its structure, and wish to make no demands on members that would detract from "doing their own thing." This lack of a common purpose has been cited by the members of one now-defunct commune as a reason for its failure:

> We weren't ready to define who we were; we certainly weren't prepared to define who we weren't—it was still just a matter of intuition. We had come together for various reasons—not overtly for a common idea or ideal, but primarily political revolutionaries . . . or just plain hermits who wanted to live in the woods. All of these different people managed to work together side by side for a while, but the fact was that there really was no shared vision.

Defining "who we are" is particularly difficult for urban communes in which members hold outside jobs. It is much easier when members work together in community jobs, as was true of all the nineteenth-century utopian communities. Some urban groups deal with this by trying to find employment as a group.

In the absence of elaborate integrating philosophies, of a sense of destiny or mission such as the religious groups have, or of an essential overriding goal, many groups develop a sense of purpose by finding shared tasks that represent a common endeavor. Construction seems to be the most important of these, for it leaves the group with a permanent monument to the shared enterprise. The end—the actual building—may not be as important for the group's identity as the means by which the buildings came about. I have experienced on many communes an infectious sense of group pride in the self-made buildings, like the gala celebration in the Connecticut Bruderhof community after the construction of new beams in the dining hall.

Rituals and shared symbols also tell a group what it is. Ritual was an important part of the life of many communes of the past, especially so for the Shakers. Every evening, each Shaker group gathered to dance, pray, and express the togetherness of the group. Many aspects of the Shaker ceremony resemble encounter group exercises in their use of energetic body movement and emotional outburst; after the ritual, one Shaker reported that the group felt "love enough to eat each other up." The Shakers also had a number of special ceremonies in which spiritual or imaginary events occurred. Some of these centered around spiritual fountains on magic hills near the villages reputedly populated by angels and spirits

—but spirits only Shakers could see, of course. Among them were such luminaries as Napoleon, George Washington, and Queen Elizabeth. Present day communes often create their own rituals, some with the same special or hidden elements that only group members share. Particularly those groups oriented around religion or mysticism find ritual an abundant source of group feeling. But even creed-less communes develop ritual. One group begins its "family meetings" by sitting in a circle and chanting "om." A number of communes use sensory-awakening or encounter exercises as a kind of ritual. In the community where I lived one summer, we arose around 6:30 and met on a grassy lawn at 7 for T'ai Chi Chuan exercises, a beautiful flowing Chinese moving meditation. For an hour before breakfast we stood in rows and moved together, all following the same pattern.

The desire for the group to become a group sometimes means that members feel a pressure to take pride only in things held in common, rather than those that belong to them separately. This, of course, was an explicit norm of the communistic groups of the last century that held all property in common (including clothes in Oneida), and found that joint ownership was an important source of community feeling. But even in "do your own thing" communes today that maintain a great deal of individual ownership and resist making demands on each other, some people still feel it important to take pride only in that which is shared. In a rural hip commune, I spoke to a woman, a particularly respected member of the commune, who had just finished building a striking looking one-room, two-level redwood house, with the help of some others in the group. It was very cleverly and artistically created, with windows that were really sculptures, framed with pieces of twisted wood found in the forest. She expressed both great pride and guilt—guilt that she should have such a nice house for her own.

The same push to take pride in what is shared rather than separate often pervades relationships. As several theorists have pointed out, groups are often threatened by exclusive relationships in their midst and desire instead diffusion of affection throughout the group.[7] Many nineteenth-century communes tended to discourage or eliminate marriage, through free love or group marriage or celibacy. Similarly, some communes today formally adopt systems of group marriage that eliminate separate, exclusive attachments. Others develop informal norms that discourage pairing-off or that exhort couples to continue their relationships with the whole group rather than isolating themselves. Members of a loosely structured, family-type "do your own thing" commune of students report that two members who formed a couple faced hostility from the others. One person said:

[7] L. Coser, "Greedy organizations," *European J. Soc.* 8 (Oct. 1967), 196–215; and P. Slater, "On social regression," *Amer. Soc. Rev.* 28 (June 1963), 339–364.

There were subtle hostilities from almost everyone being directed at their partial withdrawal from the rest of us into their own world. It came out in criticisms of their relationship by various people . . . It's true that if you start to get into a heavier-than-usual relationship with anyone, you should have every freedom to let it develop. Living in a commune, however, carries with it a responsibility to maintain a certain amount of awareness of where everyone else is at and how what you are doing is affecting the total group. If we are trying to do anything at all revolutionary and collective, we can't afford to revert to old patterns of looking out only for our own immediate needs.

A group can become a special entity if members value it above other things. Some of the nineteenth century communities eliminated the possibility of conflicting loyalties by breaking ties with the surrounding society and moving to isolated locations that the average member rarely left. But today, even for rural communities this is rarely feasible, and for urban groups it is impossible. So an important source of interpersonal friction in communes is how involved and present a member is. Meetings in which tensions and hostilities are confronted often revolve around this kind of theme. There is a dilemma here for many present-day groups, for while there may be a group pressure for involvement, there is sometimes an accompanying reluctance to make demands or to create norms that will regulate the individual's involvement—even in such simple matters as doing his share of domestic work. Yet the failure to make such norms explicit undermines the group-ness of many communes and helps lead to their dissolution. The members still feel the weight of group pressure, but there are no clear norms that pull the commune together as a group.

The reluctance to make formal rules is pervasive in the commune movement; communities such as Synanon that *do* have a highly-developed normative structure are viewed by many other communes as autocratic. There is a split among communes around the degree of organization they are willing to create. However, those that fail to organize their work and their decision-making procedures tend to find that work stays undone, some decisions never get made, and group feeling develops only with difficulty. The unwillingness to make decisions or impose order seems to be not only a function of a "do your own thing" ideology but also of a lack of trust in the group. One hip commune reported the difficulties in the group's working together on construction. ("Everything was a hassle, an object for discussion. Even how many hammer blows to use on a nail. Should it be 5 or 7?") Those communes, on the other hand, in which there is enough mutual trust and commitment to the group—often through the sense of shared purpose mentioned earlier—find that they can build organization, and that this enhances rather than detracts from their functioning as a group. In fact, I have found among residents in the very anarchic hip communes a longing for more order and group-ness than they have. A resident of Morningstar made this remark about Tolstoy Farm:

It's a groovy place. They don't let *everybody* in—just people who really believe in it. They've got some organization there. Everybody knows what he's supposed to be doing.[8]

Zablocki[9] documents the shift that many hippie communes have gone through over time, developing organization out of anarchism.

CONCLUSION

What can be said about the viability of today's commune movement? First, many of today's groups are not looking for the same kind of permanent, stable community that utopians of the past sought, so while it is true that many of today's groups are temporary and subject to much change and turnover of members, it is this kind of temporary system that some communes themselves seek. Their ideologies say that nothing should be forever, that change is part of life. On the other hand, a number of groups do wish to create long-range viable alternative communities, and to these the lessons of the past apply. Those communes that develop common purpose, an integrating philosophy, a structure for leadership and decision-making, criteria for membership and entrance procedures, organize work and property communally, affirm their bonds through ritual, and work out interpersonal difficulties through regular open confrontation have a better chance of succeeding than those that do not. They will be building commitment and also satisfying their members by creating a strong family-like group. The failure rate of communes is high, but so is the failure rate of small businesses. And no one is suggesting that small business is not a viable organizational form. As the commune movement grows, so do the number of groups that build for themselves what it takes to succeed as a commune. Part of the difference between stable and unstable, anarchistic or organized communes lies in their stage of group development. A strong commune takes time and work to develop.

* * *

An expanded discussion of the themes of this paper is found in Rosabeth Moss Kanter, *Commitment and Community: Utopias and Communes in Sociological Perspective* (Cambridge, Mass.: Harvard University Press, 1972).

8 Lamott, *op. cit.*
9 B. Zablocki, *The Joyful Community* (Baltimore: Penguin, 1971).

MOLDING

A great deal of behavioral research, in the tradition of John B. Watson and B. F. Skinner, has demonstrated the extent to which the behavior of people, like that of laboratory animals, can be selectively shaped by the judicious use of reinforcement. Whereas the reinforcers for other animals are likely to be food pellets, the reinforcers for humans are more likely to include affection, approval, and other social commodities. Other research, including the studies reported in this section, has pointed to even more subtle processes by which we mold one another. These processes center on the power of others' expectations, especially as institutionalized in systems of roles and norms, to pattern human behavior.

Robert Rosenthal and Lenore Jacobson provided a striking demonstration of the power of interpersonal expectations in the area of intellectual development. In a controlled experiment, they told teachers that some of their pupils had been identified as academic "spurters." The names of the "spurters" were actually selected from a list of random numbers. At the end of the year, however, these "spurters" in fact showed greater intellectual gains than the "non-spurters." In other words, the children whom the teachers expected to get smarter *got* smarter.

For our expectations to be effective in shaping others, they must somehow be communicated. This communication is often without words, and it is embedded in roles: sets of expectations and assumptions about how particular categories of people should and should not behave. Nancy Henley's paper closely examines one such communication system—the ways in which nonverbal cues of facial expression, gesture, and touch reinforce the prevailing patterns of dominance–submission between men and women.

People learn how they are expected to behave not only from others directly, but also from cultural prescriptions communicated through the mass media. When Philip Zimbardo and his colleagues set up a mock prison at Stanford University, the neophyte "prisoners" and "guards" experienced little difficulty in determining how they should behave. Molds for their behavior were already available from the accounts of prison life they had read and the prison movies they had seen. These patterns were strongly reinforced by the rules and arrangements of the "Stanford County Prison," which temporarily molded the "guards" into sadists and the "prisoners" into vegetables. Once the system was put into motion, it seemed to perpetuate itself, with the prisoner and guard roles complementing and thus maintaining one another.

These studies might lead one to the conclusion that people are essentially passive objects, molded like clay into various shapes and forms by their fellows and their societies. But such an analysis would be incomplete. We must recognize that we are not only the molded ones but also the molders. The expectations, roles, and institutions that pattern people's behavior and attitudes are themselves created by people. It is for each of us to decide in what ways and with what methods he wishes to mold the behavior of others.

Pygmalion in the Classroom: Teacher Expectation and Pupils' Intellectual Development

Robert Rosenthal and Lenore Jacobson

There is increasing concern over what can be done to reduce the disparities of education, of intellectual motivation and of intellectual competence that exist between the social classes and the colors of our school children. With this increasing concern, attention has focused more and more on the role of the classroom teacher, and the possible effects of her or his values, attitudes, and, especially, beliefs and expectations. Many educational theorists have expressed the opinion that the teacher's expectation of her pupils' performance may serve as an educational self-fulfilling prophecy. The teacher gets less because she expects less.

The concept of the self-fulfilling prophecy is an old idea which has found application in clinical psychology, social psychology, sociology, economics, and in everyday life. Most of the evidence for the operation of self-fulfilling prophecies has been correlational. Interpersonal prophecies have been found to agree with the behavior that was prophesied. From this, however, it cannot be said that the prophecy was the cause of its own fulfillment. The accurate prophecy may have been based on a knowledge of the prior behavior of the person whose behavior was prophesied, so that the prophecy was in a sense "contaminated" by reality. If a physician predicts a patient's improvement, we cannot say whether the doctor is only giving a sophisticated prognosis or whether the patient's improvement is based on part on the optimism engendered by the physician's prediction. If school children who perform poorly are those expected by their teachers to perform poorly, we cannot say whether the teacher's expectation was the "cause" of the pupils' poor performance, or whether the teacher's expectation was simply an accurate prognosis of performance based on her knowledge of past performance. To help answer the question raised, experiments are required in which the expectation is

---

experimentally varied and is uncontaminated by the past behavior of the person whose performance is predicted.

Such experiments have been conducted and they have shown that in behavioral research the experimenter's hypothesis may serve as self-fulfilling prophecy.[1] Of special relevance to our topic are those experiments involving allegedly bright and allegedly dull animal subjects. Half the experimenters were led to believe that their rat subjects had been specially bred for excellence of learning ability. The remaining experimenters were led to believe that their rat subjects were genetically inferior. Actually, the animals were assigned to their experimenters at random.

Regardless of whether the rat's task was to learn a maze or the appropriate responses in a Skinner box, the results were the same. Rats who were believed by their experimenters to be brighter showed learning which was significantly superior to the learning by rats whose experimenters believed them to be dull. Our best guess, supported by the experimenters' self-reports, is that allegedly well-endowed animals were handled more and handled more gently than the allegedly inferior animals. Such handling differences, along with differences in rapidity of reinforcement in the Skinner box situation, are probably sufficient to account for the differences in learning ability shown by allegedly bright and allegedly dull rats.

If rats showed superior performance when their trainer expected it, then it seemed reasonable to think that children might show superior performance when their teacher expected it. That was the reason for conducting the Oak School Experiment.

THE OAK SCHOOL EXPERIMENT

To all of the children in the Oak School, on the West Coast, the "Harvard Test of Inflected Acquisition" was administered in the Spring of 1964. This test was purported to predict academic "blooming" or intellectual growth. The reason for administering the test in the particular school was ostensibly to perform a final check of the validity of the test, a validity which was presented as already well-established. Actually, the "Harvard Test of Inflected Acquisition" was a standardized, relatively nonverbal test of intelligence, Flanagan's Tests of General Ability.

Within each of the six grades of the elementary school, there were three classrooms, one each for children performing at above-average, average, and below-average levels of scholastic achievement. In each of the 18 classrooms of the school, about 20% of the children were designated

[1] R. Rosenthal, *Experimenter Effects in Behavioral Research* (New York: Appleton-Century-Crofts, 1966).

as academic "spurters." The names of these children were reported to their new teachers in the Fall of 1964 as those who, during the academic year ahead, would show unusual intellectual gains. The "fact" of their intellectual potential was established from their scores on the test for "intellectual blooming."

Teachers were cautioned not to discuss the test findings with either their pupils or the children's parents. Actually, the names of the 20% of the children assigned to the "blooming" condition had been selected by means of a table of random numbers. The difference, then, between these children, earmarked for intellectual growth, and the undesignated control group children was in the mind of the teacher.

Four months after the teachers had been given the names of the "special" children, all the children once again took the same form of the nonverbal test of intelligence. Four months after this retest the children took the same test once again. This final retest was at the end of the school year, some eight months after the teachers had been given the expectation for intellectual growth of the special children. These retests were not explained as "retests" to the teachers, but rather as further efforts to predict intellectual growth.

The intelligence test employed, while relatively nonverbal in the sense of requiring no speaking, reading, or writing, was not entirely nonverbal. Actually there were two subtests, one requiring a greater comprehension of English—a kind of picture vocabulary test. The other subtest required less ability to understand any spoken language but more ability to reason abstractly. For shorthand purposes we refer to the former as a "verbal" subtest and to the latter as a "reasoning" subtest. The pretest correlation between these subjects was only +.42, suggesting that the two subtests were measuring somewhat different intellectual abilities.

For the school as a whole, the children of the experimental groups did not show a significantly greater gain in verbal IQ (2 points) than did the control group children. However, in total IQ (4 points) and especially in reasoning IQ (7 points) the experimental children gained more than did the control group children. In 15 of the 17 classrooms in which the reasoning IQ posttest was administered, children of the experimental group gained more than did the control group children. Even after the four-month retest this trend was already in evidence though the effects were smaller.

When we examine the results separately for the six grades we find that it was only in the first and second grades that children gained significantly more in IQ when their teacher expected it of them. In the first grade, children who were expected to gain more IQ gained over 15 points more than did the control group children. In the second grade, children who were expected to gain more IQ gained nearly 10 points more than did the control group children. In the first and second grades combined,

19% of the control group children gained 20 or more IQ points. Two-and-a-half times that many, or 47%, of the experimental group children gained 20 or more IQ points.

When educational theorists have discussed the possible effects of teachers' expectations, they have usually referred to the children at lower levels of scholastic achievement. It was interesting, therefore, to find that in the present study, children of the highest level of achievement showed as great a benefit as did the children of the lowest level of achievement of having their teachers expect intellectual gains.

At the end of the school year of this study, all teachers were asked to describe the classroom behavior of their pupils. Those children from whom intellectual growth was expected were described as having a significantly better chance of becoming successful in the future, as significantly more interesting, curious, and happy. There was a tendency, too, for these children to be seen as more appealing, adjusted, and affectionate and as lower in the need for social approval. In short, the children from whom intellectual growth was expected became more intellectually alive and autonomous—or at least were so perceived by their teachers. These findings were particularly striking among first-grade children; these were the children who had benefited most in IQ gain as a result of their teachers' favorable expectancies.

We have already seen that the children of the experimental group gained more intellectually. It was possible, therefore, that their actual intellectual growth accounted for the teachers' more favorable ratings of these children's behavior and aptitude. But a great many of the control group children also gained in IQ during the course of the year. Perhaps those who gained more intellectually among these undesignated children would also be rated more favorably by their teachers. Such was not the case. In fact, there was a tendency for teachers to rate those control group children who gained most in IQ as *less* well-adjusted, *less* interesting, and *less* affectionate than control group children who made smaller intellectual gains. From these results it would seem that when children who are expected to grow intellectually do so, they may benefit in other ways as well. When children who are not especially expected to develop intellectually do so, they may show accompanying undesirable behavior, or at least are perceived by their teachers as showing such undesirable behavior. It appears that there may be hazards to unpredicted intellectual growth.

A closer analysis of these data, broken down by whether the children were in the high, medium, or low ability tracks or groups, showed that these hazards of unpredicted intellectual growth were due primarily to the children of the low ability group. When these slow track children were in the control group, so that no intellectual gains were expected of them, they were rated less favorably by their teachers if they did show gains in IQ. The greater their IQ gains, the less favorably were they rated, both as to mental health and as to intellectual vitality. Even when the slow track children were in the experimental group, so that IQ gains were expected of them, they were not rated as favorably relative to their control group peers as were children of the high or medium track, despite the fact that they gained as much in IQ relative to the control group children as did the experimental group children of the high track. It may be difficult for a slow track child, even one whose IQ is rising, to be seen by his teacher as a well-adjusted child, or as a potentially successful child intellectually.

THE QUESTION OF MEDIATION

How did the teachers' expectations come to serve as determinants of gains in intellectual performance? The most plausible hypothesis seemed to be that children for whom unusual intellectual growth had been predicted would be attended to more by their teachers. If teachers were more attentive to the children earmarked for growth, we might expect that teachers were robbing Peter to see Paul grow. With a finite amount of time to spend with each child, if a teacher gave more time to the children of the experimental group, she would have less time to spend with the children of the control group. If the teacher's spending more time with a child led to greater intellectual gains, we could test the "robbing Peter" hypothesis by comparing the gains made by children of the experimental group with gains made by the children of the control group in each class. The robbing Peter hypothesis predicts a negative correlation. The greater the gains made by children of the experimental group (with the implication of more time spent on them) the less should be the gains made by the children of the control group (with the implication of less time spent on them). In fact, however, the correlation was positive, large, and statistically significant (+.57). The greater the gains made by children of whom gain was expected, the greater the gains made in the same classroom by those children from whom no special gain was expected.

Additional evidence that teachers did not take time from control group children to spend with the experimental group children comes from the teachers' estimates of time spent with each pupil. These estimates showed a slight tendency for teachers to spend *less* time with pupils from whom intellectual gains were expected.

That the children of the experimental group were not favored with a greater investment of time seems less surprising in view of the pattern of their greater intellectual gains. If, for example, teachers had talked to them more, we might have expected greater gains in verbal IQ. But the greater gains were found not in verbal but in reasoning IQ. It may be, of course, that the teachers were inaccurate in their estimates of time spent with each of their pupils. Possibly direct observation of the teacher-pupil interactions would have given different results, but that method was not possible in the present study. But even direct observation might not have revealed a difference in the amounts of teacher time invested in each of the two groups of children. It seems plausible to think that it was not a difference in amount of time spent with the children of the two groups which led to the differences in their rates of intellectual development. It may have been more a matter of the type of interaction which took place between the teachers and their pupils.

By what she said, by how she said it, by her facial expressions, postures, and perhaps by her touch, the teacher may have communicated to the children of the experimental group that she expected improved intellectual performance. Such communications, together with possible changes in teaching techniques, may have helped the child learn by changing his or her self-concept, expectations of his or her own behavior, motivation, as well as cognitive skills. Further research is clearly needed to narrow down the range of possible mechanisms whereby a teacher's expectations become translated into a pupil's intellectual growth. It would be valuable, for example, to have sound films of teachers interacting with their pupils. We might then look for differences in the ways teachers interact with those children from whom they expect more intellectual growth compared to those from whom they expect less. On the basis of films of psychological experimenters interacting with subjects from whom different responses were expected, we know that even in such highly standardized situations, unintentional communications can be subtle and complex.[2] How much more subtle and complex may be the communications between children and their teachers in the less highly standardized classroom situation.

CONCLUSIONS

The results of the Oak School experiment provide further evidence that one person's expectations of another's behavior may serve as a self-fulfilling prophecy. When teachers expected that certain children would show greater intellectual development, those children did show greater intellectual development. A number of more recent experiments have provided additional evidence for the operation of teacher expectancy effects, in contexts ranging from the classroom to teaching athletic skills. Although not all of the studies that have been conducted show such effects, a large proportion of them do.[3]

It may be that as teacher training institutions acquaint teachers-to-be with the possibility that their expectations of their pupils' performance

[2] R. Rosenthal, "Covert communication in the psychological experiment," *Psychological Bulletin*, 1967, 67, 356–367.

[3] R. Rosenthal, "Teacher expectation and pupil learning," in R. D. Strom (Ed.), *Teachers and the Learning Process* (Englewood Cliffs, N.J.: Prentice-Hall, 1971).

may serve as self-fulfilling prophecies, these teacher trainees may be given a new expectancy—that children can learn more than they had believed possible.

Perhaps the most suitable summary of the hypothesis discussed in this paper has already been written. The writer is George Bernard Shaw, the play is "Pygmalion," and the speaker is Eliza Doolittle:

> "You see, really and truly, . . . the difference between a lady and a flower girl is not how she behaves, but how she's treated. I shall always be a flower girl to Professor Higgins, because he . . . treats me as a flower girl, . . . but I know I can be a lady to you, because you always treat me as a lady, and always will."

* * *

An expanded discussion of self-fulfilling prophecies and a full account of the Oak School experiment are presented in Robert Rosenthal and Lenore Jacobson, *Pygmalion in the Classroom: Teacher Expectation and Pupils' Intellectual Development* (New York: Holt, Rinehart and Winston, 1968).

Power, Sex, and Nonverbal Communication

Nancy M. Henley

In front of, and defending, the larger political-economic structure that determines our lives and defines the context of human relationships, there is a micropolitical structure that helps maintain it. The "trivia" of everyday life—using "sir" or first name, touching others, dropping the eyes, smiling, interrupting, and so on—that characterize these micropolitics are commonly understood as facilitators of social intercourse, but are not recognized as defenders of the status quo—of the state, of the wealthy, of authority, of all those whose power may be challenged. Nevertheless, these minutiae find their place on a continuum of social control which extends from internalized socialization (the colonization of the mind) at the one end to sheer physical force (guns, clubs, incarceration) at the other.

Micropolitical cues are, moreover, of particular importance in the study of woman's place in our society, for several reasons. First, like any other oppressed group, women should know all the chains binding them. Second, women are likely targets for this subtle form of social control for two reasons: they are particularly socialized to docility and passivity, and their physical integration around centers of power (as wives, secretaries, etc.) ensures their frequent interaction (verbal and nonverbal) with those in power. Finally, women are more sensitive than men to social cues in general, as many studies have shown, and to nonverbal cues in particular.

This paper will seek to examine certain nonverbal behaviors, and some subtle verbal ones, in their social context as a step toward understanding the myriad faces of power.

Abridged from *Berkeley Journal of Sociology*, 1973, *18*, 1–26.

SEXUAL DIMORPHISM OR UNIMORPHISM?

From the beginning we should guard against the mistake of assuming that the observed nonverbal (or verbal) differences between the human sexes result from biology. In 1943 Galt pointed out humanity's long journey from an apparently little-acknowledged distinction between the sexes (and early bisexuality and natural "polymorphous perversity") to the present "Western" cultural assumption of extreme sexual distinction (and narrowly channeled sexuality). He writes,

> . . . it should be clear that the *either-or* type of sexual behavior demanded of man and woman by the mores of Western culture under threat of severe penalty is not in line with the trend of sexual adjustment as it has developed throughout biological evolution.[1]

Birdwhistell writes that when different animal species are rated on a spectrum by the extent of their sexual dimorphism, on the basis of secondary sexual characteristics "man seems far closer to the unimorphic end of the spectrum than he might like to believe." [2] He states that his work in kinesics leads him to postulate "that man and probably a number of other weakly dimorphic species necessarily organize much of gender display and recognition at the level of position, movement, and expression." Thus we must realize that much of our nonverbal behavior, far from being "natural," has been developed and modified to emphasize and display sex differences, much like our manner of dress. (Class differences are signaled and emphasized in these ways too.)

COMMUNICATION—VERBAL AND NONVERBAL

Our culture emphasizes verbal over nonverbal communication. English is taught in our schools through all grades, with the aims of both better understanding (diagramming sentences, learning Latin roots) and better expression (writing compositions). Nonverbal communication isn't taught: we never learn to analyze what certain postures, gestures, and looks mean, or how to express ourselves better nonverbally. (Of course, nonverbal communication is learned informally, just as language is learned before we enter schools to study it.) This doesn't mean everybody doesn't *know* that looks and postures mean something, perhaps every-

[1] W. E. Galt, "The Male-Female Dichotomy in Human Behavior," *Psychiatry*, VI (1943), p. 9.

[2] R. L. Birdwhistell, *Kinesics and Context: Essays on Body Motion Communication* (Philadelphia, 1970), pp. 41, 42.

thing, especially in emotion-charged interaction. But mentioning looks and postures is illegitimate in reporting communication; legal transcripts and newspaper accounts don't record them. And they are seldom allowed in personal argument ("What look? What tone of voice? Look, did I say OK, or didn't I?").

Yet, with all our ignorance about nonverbal communication, the evidence is that the nonverbal message greatly overpowers the verbal one; one estimate is that it carries 4.3 times the weight. In the face of the facts that nonverbal communication is more important than verbal, that it helps maintain the power structure, that women are particularly influenced by it, and that it is glaringly ignored in our education and disallowed in argument, it becomes important for all those deprived of power, and particularly women, to learn all they can about how it affects their lives, and to apply that knowledge to their struggle for liberation.

Most of the literature on nonverbal communication emphasizes solidarity relations (friendship, liking, attraction) rather than power relations. But insights into the status aspects of nonverbal communication are provided by the anecdotal descriptions of writers like Goffman and Haley. Haley in a well-known essay discusses "The Art of Psychoanalysis" from the point of view of gamesmanship. He notes the importance of the physical aspects of this status-laden interaction:

> By placing the patient on a couch, the analyst gives the patient the feeling of having his feet up in the air and the knowledge that the analyst has both feet on the ground. Not only is the patient disconcerted by having to lie down while talking, but he finds himself literally below the analyst and so his one-down position is geographically emphasized. In addition, the analyst seats himself behind the couch where he can watch the patient but the patient cannot watch him. This gives the patient the sort of disconcerted feeling a person has when sparring with an opponent while blindfolded. Unable to see what response his ploys provoke, he is unsure when he is one-up and one-down. . . . Another purpose is served by the position behind the couch. Inevitably what the analyst says becomes exaggerated in importance since the patient lacks any other means of determining his effect on the analyst.[3]

Goffman, in his intriguing essay "The Nature of Deference and Demeanor," points to many characteristics associated with status. "Between superordinate and subordinate," he writes, "we may expect to find asymmetrical relations, the superordinate having the right to exercise certain familiarities which the subordinate is not allowed to reciprocate."[4] Goffman cites such familiarities as using familiar address, asking for personal information, touching, teasing, and informal demeanor.

The relation of nonverbal cues to the exercise of power is complex.

[3] J. Haley, "The Art of Psychoanalysis," in S. I. Hayakawa, *The Use and Misuse of Language* (Greenwich, Conn., 1962), pp. 209–210.

[4] E. Goffman, *Interaction Ritual* (New York, 1967), p. 64.

On a simple behavioral level, we may observe first that they are *associated* with power or the lack of it. Further they may *affect* the power relationship, for example, when in an established relationship a dominance gesture is not met with submission. On an analytical level, we may decide that the gestures act as cues *symbolic* of power, both to display for observers and to *express* for both sender and receiver the power relation. On a theoretical level, we may suggest that nonverbal behaviors are used overall to *maintain* the power relations of a society, but in individual situations may help *establish* such relations, as when people in a competitive situation begin to seek dominance over each other. For the most part this article will deal with the association between behavior and status in the maintenance of social structure.

SUBTLE ASPECTS OF LANGUAGE

Although we are focusing on nonverbal communication, we know that language also carries messages of status in its structure and usage. Sociolinguists have for some years pursued political, class, and status aspects of language, but until recently only feminists looked into ("complained about") sexism in our language.

SPEECH

Austin has commented on sex and status differences in speech:

> In our culture little boys tend to be nasal . . . and little girls, oral. Nasality is considered 'tough' and 'vulgar' and is somewhat discouraged by elders. 'Gentlemanly' little boys tend to be oral also. . . . A 'little girl's voice' (innocence, helplessness, regression) is composed of high pitch and orality.
>
> The dominant middle-class white culture in the United States has certain set views on lower-class Negro speech. It is 'loud,' 'unclear,' 'slurred,' 'lazy.' The myth of loudness should be exorcised at once. Any minority or 'out-group' is characterized as 'loud'—Americans in Europe, Englishmen in America, and so on.[5]

When considering women as the out-group, at first it may seem that the characterization "loud" does not apply: their speech is renowned as soft, quiet (the "lady's" speech is golden). However, only the acceptable members of the out-group (i.e., those allowed into some legitimate relationship with the in-group) are identified as having the in-group characteristics and are not stereotyped as loud. Non-ladies are often characterized by their loudness, and female advocates of women's liberation are used to being described as "shrill." Of course, the word *shrill* simply adds the connotation of loudness to that of high pitch (commonly associated with the female voice, though not determined by biology).

[5] W. M. Austin, "Some Social Aspects of Paralanguage," *Canadian Journal of Linguistics,* XI (1965), pp. 34, 37, 38.

TERMS OF ADDRESS

The use of different terms of address is one very familiar distinction made with language. Inferiors must address superiors by title and last name (Mr., Dr., Professor Jones) or by other polite address, such as "sir," or polite second-person forms (*vous, Sie, usted*) in languages which have them. Superiors may address inferiors by first name or by the familiar form (*tu, du, tú*). Brown and his colleagues have demonstrated how terms of address are used to indicate both status and solidarity relations: status is characterized by asymmetry of address as described above, and solidarity by symmetric use of familiar (close) or polite (distant) address. Historically the polite form has been used symmetrically within the upper classes, and the familiar form symmetrically within the lower classes.

In a detailed analysis of the status and solidarity dimensions of interpersonal relationships, Brown has gone beyond the terms of address to a generalization of the rules that govern their use; this generalization applies to other forms of communicative behavior we will examine later. He has pointed out a universal norm in terms of address that has the generalized formula: "If form X is used to inferiors it is used between intimates, and if form Y is used to superiors it is used between strangers."[6] Furthermore, when there is a clear difference of status between two persons, the right to initiate a change to more intimate forms of relationship (e.g., mutual first name or familiar address) belongs to the superior.

SELF-DISCLOSURE

Goffman writes:

> . . . in American business organizations the boss may thoughtfully ask the elevator man how his children are, but this entrance into another's life may be blocked to the elevator man, who can appreciate the concern but not return it. Perhaps the clearest form of this is found in the psychiatrist-patient relation, where the psychiatrist has the right to touch on aspects of the patient's life that the patient might not even allow himself to touch upon, while of course this privilege is not reciprocated.[7]

A study of address and social relations in a business organization confirms both the basic analysis of address made by Brown and the observations about self-disclosure made by Goffman. Individuals in the company studied were "more self-disclosing to their immediate superior than to their immediate subordinates";[8] that is, personal information flows op-

[6] R. Brown, *Social Psychology* (Glencoe, Ill., 1965), p. 92.

[7] Goffman, *op. cit.*, p. 64.

[8] D. I. Slobin, S. H. Miller, L. W. Porter, "Forms of Address and Social Relations in a Business Organization," *Journal of Personality and Social Psychology,* VIII (1968), p. 292.

posite to the flow of authority. This finding may be juxtaposed with that of Jourard and Lasakow, who found that females disclose themselves more to others than do males. Although this effect has been frequently replicated, a number of studies have failed to find sex differences in self-disclosure; however, no study has reported greater male disclosure.

The whole question of the relation of self-disclosure to status, and its special importance for women, is further illuminated in comparing the controlled aura of the professional or VIP (doctor, corporation head, judge) with the more variable demeanor of ordinary people, particularly children, working class people, women, and persons of "ethnic" background.

"Cool" is nothing more than the withholding of information, that is, refusing to disclose one's thoughts and emotions, and the value it gives to street people, poker players, and psychiatrists is of the same sort. But while it is practically a class characteristic for the upper classes, for lower-class people it can only be an individual or situational variable. Disadvantaged people find it difficult to withhold personal information; poor people and national minorities are forced to reveal any information about themselves that is wanted by the authorities. They are the focus of endless questioning by social workers and government officials, and of endless investigation by anthropologists and sociologists. The cultures of most poor and "ethnic" peoples in our societies, and those of women and children, allow for a broader and deeper range of emotional display than that of adult white males, and members of those cultures are commonly depicted as "uncontrolled" emotionally. Male children are socialized away from this, but the socialization of female children to be more expressive emotionally sets them up for their vulnerability as "emotional" women, with little control over the visibility of their affect.

NONVERBAL COMMUNICATION

DEMEANOR

In the area of demeanor, Goffman observes that in hospital staff meetings, "medical doctors had the privilege of swearing, changing the topic of conversation, and sitting in undignified positions," [9] while attendants were required to show greater circumspection. Furthermore, doctors' freedom to lounge on the nursing station counter and to joke with the nurses could be extended to other ranks only after it had been initiated by doctors.

The rules of demeanor recognized by Goffman may also be examined with special reference to women: women, too, are denied such privileges

[9] Goffman, *op. cit.*, p. 78.

as swearing and sitting in undignified positions, which are allowed to men, and are explicitly required to be more circumspect than men by all standards, including the well-known double one.

SPACE

There are silent messages in the nonhuman environment as well as the human one, and the distribution of space is one carrier of such messages. The imposing height and space of courtrooms and governmental buildings intimidate, as they are meant to, the people whose lives are affected there. A store-front structure is designed to draw people in; a courthouse or library, with distant stone facade and discouraging high steps, is designed to turn people away.

Brown discusses spatial relations (as one of five types of interpersonal relationship) in terms of solidarity and status dimensions, noting that status differences are marked by being above or below, in front or behind. Sommer observes that dominant animals and human beings have a larger envelope of inviolability surrounding them than do subordinate ones (dominants may not be approached as closely). Sex status in the unequal distribution of personal space is demonstrated in a study reported by Willis. He found, in studying the initial speaking distance set by an approaching person, that women were approached more closely than were men, by both men and women.

TOUCH

Both popular writers and psychological researchers who have written on touching have generally advanced sexual explanations for it, or see it only in a context of intimacy.

But there are clearly status connotations in touching, and it will be valuable to consider the touching between the sexes in this light. Goffman writes of the "touch system" in a hospital: "The doctors touched other ranks as a means of conveying friendly support and comfort, but other ranks tended to feel that it would be presumptuous for them to reciprocate a doctor's touch, let alone initiate such a contact with a doctor." [10]

Touching is also one of the closer invasions of one's personal space, and may be related to the deference shown the space surrounding the body. It is even more a physical threat than space violation, pointing, or staring, perhaps a vestige of the days when dominance was determined by physical prowess. The status dimension of touching is illustrated in the following interactions between pairs of persons of differing status (which would be more likely to put an arm around the shoulder, a hand on the back, tap the chest, or hold the wrists?): teacher and student; master and servant; policeman and accused; doctor and patient; minister and parish-

[10] Goffman, *op. cit.*, p. 74.

ioner; counselor and client; foreman and worker; businessman and secretary.

Even those who put forward a sexual explanation for males' touching of females have to admit that there is at least a status overlay: female factory workers, secretaries, students, servants, and waitresses are often unwillingly felt or pinched, but women of higher status (e.g., "boss ladies," "first ladies," and "ladies" in general) aren't.

In fact, women are expected to accept as normal behavior the daily violations of their persons. However, when they reciprocate or, especially, initiate touch with men they are likely to be interpreted as conveying specific sexual intent.

What investigation of touching there has been by psychologists provides evidence in support of the thesis that females are touched by others more than males are. Studies of child-mother interaction have reported greater touching of female than of male children, at least from age six months on.

It is interesting to examine some of the consequences of being handled more as a child. Lewis puts forward the thesis "that the major socialization process, in terms of attachment or social behavior, is to move the infant from a proximal mode of social interaction [e.g., touching, rocking, holding] to a distal mode [e.g., smiling and vocalizing]." [11] His data suggest that boys are moved faster from the proximal to distal form of interaction than girls are, and indeed, that girls are never socialized as thoroughly as boys in this regard, i.e., to distal relations, associated with more independence. Thus, greater touching of females is part of the larger picture in which they are socialized to dependence, to be not the manipulators of their environment, but the objects in it.

An observational study by this author investigated touching with regard to several status dimensions (socioeconomic status, sex, and age) and found that in all these cases those of higher status (higher SES, male, older) touched those of lower status significantly more. The pattern of touching between and within the sexes was particularly striking when other factors were held constant, i.e., when women did not have other status advantages in the absence of the sex one. The greater frequency of touching between the sexes, when compared to within sexes, may suggest components of both heterosexual attraction and homosexual inhibition. However, sexual attraction is not sufficient to explain men's greater touching of women since it would predict that women would touch men as frequently. It can hardly be claimed any longer that men have greater "sex drives," therefore a lesser expression of sex must be attributed to an inhibition on the part of women to display sexual interest in this manner. At this point we are back where we started: the question becomes one of

11 M. Lewis, "Parents and Children: Sex-Role Development," *School Review*, LXXX (1972), p. 234.

why one sex feels free to express its motivation tactually and the other does not. The status difference, which is a common variable underlying the differential utilization of touch in other status dimensions, best explains the difference in touching between the sexes.

The hypothesis that touch communicates power is not necessarily in conflict with an alternative interpretation that it communicates intimacy. There is no question that persons who are close exchange touch more. Touch may be regarded as a nonverbal equivalent of calling another by first name; used reciprocally, it indicates solidarity; when nonreciprocal, it indicates status. Even when there is mutuality, however, we may note that there is some indication of status difference. Consider, for example, who, over the course of dating by a couple, initiates touching: usually the male is the first to place his arm around the female, rather than vice versa.

EYE CONTACT

Perhaps the most extensively researched area in nonverbal communication is that of eye contact. And according to one researcher: "Perhaps the most powerful single variable [in eye contact] is sex." [12] There is, first of all, a common finding that in interactions, women look more at the other person than do men. Women also have a higher percentage of mutual looking.

It is important to put eye contact into its political context, taking into account the importance of social approval to women's survival. The hypothesis that "subjects maintain more eye contact with individuals toward whom they have developed higher expectancies for social approval" was supported in Efran and Broughton's study of visual interaction in males.[13] And Exline writes: "Women . . . may look at other persons more than do men because they value more highly the kinds of information they can obtain through such activity." [14] More pointedly, Rubin suggests that "gazing may serve as a vehicle of emotional expression for women and, in addition, may allow women to obtain cues from their male partners concerning the appropriateness of their behavior." [15]

There is another reason for women's greater eye contact: the listener in a conversation tends to look at the speaker rather than vice versa, and men tend to talk more than women.

[12] S. Duncan, "Nonverbal Communication," *Psychological Bulletin,* LXII (1969), p. 129.

[13] J. S. Efran and A. Broughton, "Effect of Expectancies for Social Approval on Visual Behavior," *Journal of Personality and Social Psychology,* IV (1966), pp. 103–107.

[14] See: R. Exline, "Explorations in the Process of Person Perception: Visual Interaction in Relation to Competition, Sex, and Need for Affiliation," *Journal of Personality,* XXXI (1963), p. 18.

[15] Z. Rubin, "Measurement of Romantic Love," *Journal of Personality and Social Psychology,* XVI (1970), p. 272.

Dominance may also be communicated through eye contact (with other nonverbal cues), as illustrated by O'Connor in this account:

A husband and wife are at a party. The wife says something that the husband does not want her to say. . . . He quickly tightens the muscles around his jaw and gives her a rapid but intense direct stare. . . . The wife, who is acutely sensitive to the gestures of the man on whom she is dependent, immediately stops the conversation, lowers or turns her head slightly, averts her eyes or gives off some other gesture of submission which communicates acquiescence to her husband and reduces his aggression.[16]

Research reported by Ellsworth, Carlsmith, and Henson supports the notion that the stare can be perceived as an aggressive gesture. These authors write: "The studies reported here demonstrate that staring at humans can elicit the same sort of responses that are common in primates; that is, staring can act like a primate threat display."[17] The suggestion that the averted glance may be a gesture of submission is supported by the research of Hutt and Ounsted, who compare human gaze aversion to "appeasement postures" in birds.

There seems to be some discrepancy between the notions that dominance is established or maintained by the nonmutual glance, and that women do more looking. But there are several factors that resolve this conflict. First, of course, we must remember that a greater portion of women's looking consists of *mutual* eye contact. Also, women may look at the other more and still not use nonmutual looking to dominate, by looking when another is speaking (an act outside the realm of competition). They may, furthermore, be the first to look away (the submissive gesture) when mutual glance is maintained for some while. More detailed research on sex differences in the initiation and termination of eye contact, in coordination with speaking patterns, would further our understanding here.

VISIBILITY

Visibility is related to both eye contact and self-disclosure: it is the availability of (visual) information about oneself to others, with all the power that information conveys. Further insight into the politics of visibility is given by Michael Argyle and his colleagues. In one study they presented the idea that if one person in an encounter is less visible than another, that person dominates the encounter; their data supported this hypothesis. We think immediately of police interrogation, or of the therapeutic situation described by Jay Haley. Visibility also affects the sexes

[16] L. O'Connor, "Male Dominance: The Nitty Gritty of Oppression," *It Ain't Me Babe*, I (1970), p. 9.

[17] P. C. Ellsworth, J. M. Carlsmith, and A. Henson, "The Stare as a Stimulus to Flight in Human Subjects: A Series of Field Experiments," *Journal of Personality and Social Psychology*, XXI (1972), p. 310.

differently: females, for instance, were made particularly uncomfortable when they could not see the other person in an interview.

In another study, Argyle and Williams[18] found that subjects in an interview situation were more likely to feel themselves to be "observed" rather than "observer" when they were being interviewed (as opposed to interviewing), were younger, were female, and if female, were with a male. The authors suggested that in a male-female encounter, the female is cast in her traditional role of "performer" and therefore feels more observed than does the male.

In a society in which women's clothing is designed explicitly to reveal the body and its contours; in which women are ogled, whistled at, and pinched while simply going about their business; in which they see advertisements in magazines, on billboards, on TV in their own homes, showing revealingly-clad women; in which tactual information about them is freely available, their bodies accessible to touch like community property; in which even their marital status is the first information by which a stranger identifies them—in such a society it is little wonder that women feel "observed." They are.

GESTURES OF DOMINANCE AND SUBMISSION

Dominant and submissive gestures have long been described by students of animal behavior, often with some reference to their similarity to the gestures of human beings. We noted earlier that the direct stare has been characterized as a threat, and the averted glance as a sign of submission, among humans. O'Connor describes some subtle distinctions that make a gesture submissive rather than dominant:

> Women use [the direct stare] as well as men, but often in modified form. While looking directly at a man, a woman usually has her head slightly tilted, implying the beginning of a presenting gesture or enough submission to render the stare ambivalent if not actually submissive.[19]

Staring, pointing, and touching may be considered as dominance gestures with the corresponding submissive gestures being, respectively, lowering or averting the eyes, stopping action or speech, and cuddling to the touch. Smiling is another recognized submissive gesture, the badge of women and of the shuffling Tom.

Interruption may also be considered a dominance gesture, and allowing interruption, the corresponding submissive gesture. Our own conversational experiences will confirm that superiors can more readily interrupt others, and more readily resist interruption by others, than subordinates.

[18] M. Argyle and M. Williams, "Observer or Observed? A Reversible Perspective in Person Perception," *Sociometry*, XXXII (1969), pp. 396–412.

[19] O'Connor, *op. cit.*, p. 9.

WHEN POWER BECOMES SEX: VIOLATION OF SEX STATUS NORMS

We noted earlier that women's touch was more likely to be interpreted as having sexual intent than men's. Similarly, women's stare, physical closeness, and loosening of demeanor may all be taken by men as sexual invitations. Other characteristics that are associated with men, such as a husky voice or the withholding of information (the "woman of mystery"), are considered sexy in women. We have seen that these behaviors and characteristics are not just "natural" or pointless properties in men, but carry status and power connotations, helping maintain their place in the social order. Why should these concomitants of status lose those connotations, and in addition, take on sexual connotations, when used by the wrong sex? It is because the implication of power is unacceptable when the actor is a woman, and therefore must be denied.

Sex is a convenient alternative interpretation because (a) many of these behaviors—touching, gazing, proximity, and relaxed demeanor—are also expressive of solidarity and intimacy, and appropriate to a sexual relationship; and (b) attribution of sexual aggressiveness to a woman both compliments the man and disarms the woman, and places her back in her familiar unthreatening role as sex object (as in "You're so cute when you're mad, baby."). There are other ways in which women are put down for exhibiting "male" characteristics: they are labeled deviant and abhorrent (castrating, domineering), or lesbian.

CONCLUSION

We have noted the importance of nonverbal and subtle verbal cues in the maintenance of the social structure and of power relationships, and their particular importance in restricting women to "their" place. In grammar, vocabulary, voice quality, and intonation patterns, women's language keeps them at a disadvantage, while men's (the dominant) language tends to ignore women completely or deprecate them. Terms of address, conversational patterns, self-disclosure, demeanor, distribution of space, touch, eye contact, and visibility all contribute to the maintenance of the status quo. The accessibility of information about subordinate persons and groups, including women, is used to subordinate and subdue them.

When subordinate groups defy the norms governing micropolitical acts, authority's first attempt at control is the denial of the norm violation, and substitution of an interpretation (for women, sexual aggression) which re-establishes the former relationship. The dual nature of many of the signals, used differently as indicators of either status or solidarity, makes them particularly available for this ploy.

The findings presented here have certain implications for women and others in inferior positions who wish to counteract the power expressed over them. They may begin to become conscious of the nonverbal symbolism of power, in order to resist it when it is used by others to exert control, and to exercise it themselves to help reverse the power relationships in their environment. Similarly, those reluctantly in positions of power, like men who wish to divest themselves of "foreskin privilege," can begin to monitor their own acts toward others and their reactions to others' acts, in an attempt to exorcise the subtle power indicators from their daily interactions.

Manipulating these status cues will not, of course, change the fundamental power relationships in our society. Knowledge of them will, however, raise consciousness and enable people to detect the subtle ways in which they are inhibited, coerced, and controlled.

The Psychology of Imprisonment: Privation, Power, and Pathology

Philip G. Zimbardo, Craig Haney,
W. Curtis Banks, and David Jaffe

In prison, those things withheld from and denied to the prisoner become precisely what he wants most of all.

ELDRIDGE CLEAVER, *Soul on Ice* (1968)

Our sense of power is more vivid when we break a man's spirit than when we win his heart.

ERIC HOFFER, *The Passionate State of Mind* (1954)

Every prison that men build is built with bricks of shame, and bound with bars lest Christ should see how men their brothers maim.

OSCAR WILDE, *The Ballad of Reading Gaol* (1898)

Wherever any one is against his will, that is to him a prison.

EPICTETUS, *Discourses* (2nd cent.)

The quiet of a summer Sunday morning in Palo Alto, California was shattered by a screeching squad car siren as police swept through the city picking up college students in a surprise mass arrest. Each suspect was charged with a felony, warned of his constitutional rights, spread-eagled against the car, searched, handcuffed and carted off in the back seat of the squad car to the police station for booking. In some cases, curious neighbors who witnessed these arrests expressed sympathy and concern to the families of these unfortunate young men. Said one alarmed mother of an 18-year-old college sophomore arrested for armed robbery,

"I felt my son must have done something; the police have come to get my son!"

After being fingerprinted and having identification forms prepared for his "jacket" (central information file), each prisoner was left isolated in a detention cell to wonder what he had done to get himself into this mess. After a while, he was blindfolded and transported to the "Stanford County Prison." Here he began the induction process of becoming a prisoner—stripped naked, skin searched, deloused, and issued a uniform, bedding, soap and towel. By late afternoon when nine such arrests had been completed, these youthful "first offenders" sat in dazed silence on the cots in their barren cells trying to make sense out of these unexpected events which had transformed their lives so dramatically. Something out of the ordinary was taking place; not the routine police arrests and processing which were executed with customary detached efficiency, nor the condition of being incarcerated behind metal bars in overcrowded cells with total strangers. There were however, some things which didn't fit, which forced each inmate to wonder just what kind of prison this was that he had gotten himself into and what would he have to go through before he was eventually released or transferred to another prison.

* * *

We're all of us guinea pigs in the laboratory of God.
Humanity is just a work in progress.

TENNESSEE WILLIAMS, *Camino Real*

These men were part of a very unusual kind of prison, an experimental or mock prison, created by social psychologists for the purpose of intensively studying the effects of imprisonment upon volunteer research subjects. When we planned our two-week long simulation of prison life, we were primarily concerned about understanding the process by which people adapt to the novel and alien environment in which those called "prisoners" lose their liberty, civil rights, independence and privacy, while those called "guards" gain social power by accepting the responsibility for controlling and managing the lives of their dependent charges.

The decision to investigate this and related issues in the context of a mock prison rather than an actual one was based upon two premises. Prison systems are fortresses of secrecy, closed to impartial observation, and thereby immune to critical analysis from anyone not already part of the correctional authority. It is virtually impossible even for congressional investigating committees to have extended, truly open access to daily prison operations; for individual citizens the likelihood is considerably less. Secondly, in any real prison, it is impossible to separate out what each individual brings into the prison from what the prison brings out in each person. When observing, for instance, a given act of violence or brutality in a prison setting, it is impossible to determine whether it is attributable to some aspect of the situation or to preexisting personality characteristics of the special population of those who become prisoners and guards.

By populating our mock prison entirely with a homogeneous group of individuals judged to be "normal-average" on a variety of personality dimensions, we were better able to assess the impact of acute situational forces upon the resulting behavior, uncontaminated by chronic personality traits typically used to "explain" prison incidents.

Our final sample of participants (10 prisoners and 11 guards) were selected from over 75 volunteers recruited through ads in the city and campus newspapers. The applicants were mostly college students from all over the United States and Canada who happened to be in the Stanford area during the summer and were attracted by the lure of earning $15 a day for participating in a study of prison life. All applicants were given an intensive clinical interview and completed an extensive background questionnaire, and we selected only those who were judged to be emotionally stable, physically healthy, mature, law-abiding citizens.

This sample of average, middle-class, Caucasian college males (there was one Oriental student) was then arbitrarily divided into two subgroups by a flip of the coin. Half were randomly assigned to role-play being guards, the others to be prisoners. Thus, there were no measurable differences between the guards and the prisoners at the start of this experiment. Although initially warned that as prisoners their privacy and other civil rights would be violated and they might be subjected to harassment, every subject was completely confident in his ability to endure whatever the prison had to offer for the full two-week experimental period. Armed with this illusion of personal invulnerability and autonomy, each subject unhesitatingly agreed to give his "informed consent" to participate. It is important to note in passing that the primary motivation which got these subjects into this mock prison is similar to that which gets most other men into real prisons—the chance to make some easy money.

* * *

We are aware of the content of experience, but
unaware that it is illusion.
We see the shadows, but take them for substance.

R. D. LAING, *Self and Others*

What was most surprising about the outcome of this simulated prison experience was the ease with which sadistic behavior could be elicited from quite normal young men, and the contagious spread of emotional pathology among those carefully selected precisely for their emotional stability. Perhaps even more astonishing to us was the permeability of the boundaries between reality and delusion, between self-identity and situational role. What began as a simple academic exercise gradually became a force of monstrous proportion, generating unpredictable consequences in all those who came within the walls of this special prison. But that is getting ahead of our story, to which we return for the warden's impromptu welcome to his new inmates:

As you probably already know I'm your Warden. All of you have shown that you are unable to function outside in the real world for one reason or another —that somehow you lack a responsibility of good citizens of this great country. We of this prison, your correctional staff, are going to help you learn what your responsibilities as citizens of this country are. Here are the rules. Sometime in the very near future there will be a copy of the rules posted in each of the cells. We expect you to know them and to be able to recite them by number. If you follow all of these rules and keep your hands clean, repent for your misdeeds and show a proper attitude of penitence, you and I will get along just fine.

There followed a reading off of the sixteen basic rules of prisoner conduct (which the warden and his staff of correctional officers had previously compiled):

Rule Number One: Prisoners must remain silent during rest periods, after lights out, during meals, and whenever they are outside the prison yard. Two: Prisoners must eat at mealtimes and only at mealtimes. Three: Prisoners must not move, tamper, deface or damage walls, ceilings, windows, doors, or other prison property . . . Seven: Prisoners must address each other by their ID number only. Eight: Prisoners must address the guards as "Mr. Correctional Officer" . . . Sixteen: Failure to obey any of the above rules may result in punishment.

The prison was physically constructed in the basement of Stanford University's psychology building, which was deserted after the end of the summer school session. A long corridor was converted into the prison "Yard" by partitioning off both ends. Three small laboratory rooms opening onto this corridor were made into cells by replacing their doors with metal barred ones and replacing existing furniture with three cots to a cell. Adjacent offices were refurnished as guards' quarters, interview-testing rooms, and bedrooms for the "Warden" (Jaffe) and the "Superintendent" (Zimbardo). A concealed video camera and hidden microphones recorded much of the verbal and nonverbal interactions between and among guards and prisoners. The physical environment was one in which prisoners could always be observed by the staff, the only exception being when they were secluded in solitary confinement (a small, dark storage closet, labelled "The Hole").

Our mock prison represented an attempt to simulate *functionally* some of the significant features of the psychological state of imprisonment. We did not intend to generate a literal simulation of "real" prison details or standard operational practices. Rather, our primary concern was to achieve some equivalent psychological effects despite differences between the form and structure of the particular operations employed in the "Stanford County Prison" and those in "real" prisons.

"Real" prisoners typically report feeling powerless, arbitrarily controlled, dependent, frustrated, hopeless, anonymous, dehumanized, and emasculated. It is not possible, pragmatically or ethically, to create such chronic states in volunteer subjects who realize that they are in an experiment for only a short time. Racism, physical brutality, indefinite confinement, and enforced homosexuality were not features of our mock prison. Instead, we created symbolic manifestations of those variables presumably fundamental to the experience of being imprisoned.

Anonymity was promoted through a variety of operations to minimize each prisoner's uniqueness and prior identity. Their uniforms, ID numbers, and nylon stocking caps, as well as removal of their personal effects and being housed in barren cells, all made the subjects appear similar to each other, often indistinguishable to observers, and forced upon them the situational group identity of "prisoner." Having to wear smocks, which were like dresses, without undergarments caused the prisoners to be more restrained in their physical actions and to move in ways which were more feminine than masculine. Forcing the prisoners to obtain permission from the guards for routine and simple activities such as writing letters, smoking a cigarette, or even going to the toilet elicited from them a child-like dependency.

Above all, "real" prisons are time machines for playing tricks with the human conception of time. In our windowless prison, the prisoners often did not even know whether it was day or night, or what hour it was. A few hours after falling asleep, they were rousted by shrill whistles for their "count." Over the course of the study, the duration of the counts was gradually and spontaneously increased by the guards from their initial perfunctory ten minutes to a seemingly interminable several hours. During these interactions, guards who were bored could find ways to amuse themselves, recalcitrant prisoners could be ridiculed, arbitrary rules could be enacted, and any dissension among the prisoners could be openly exaggerated by the guards.

The guards were also "deindividuated" by virtue of wearing identical khaki uniforms and silver reflector sunglasses which made eye contact with them impossible. Their symbols of power were billy clubs, whistles, handcuffs, and the keys to the cells and the "main gate." Although our guards received no formal training from us in how to be guards, for the most part they moved with apparent ease into their roles. Movies, TV, novels, and all of our mass media had already provided them with ample models of prison guards to emulate. Just as do "real" correctional officers subjected to these very same cultural influences, our mock guards had available to them behavioral templates of what it means to be a guard, upon which they could improvise their role performances. So too, our mock prisoners had already learned to some extent from mass media and selected life experiences what were appropriate prisoner reactions.

Because we were as interested in the guards' behavior as in the prisoners', they were given considerable latitude for improvisation and for developing strategies and tactics of prisoner management. For the bulk of the time guards and prisoners interacted on the yard alone without the presence of any higher-ups. Our guards were told that they must maintain "law and order" in this prison, that they were responsible for handling any trouble which might break out, and they were cautioned as to the seriousness and potential dangers of the situation they were about to enter. Surprisingly, in most prison systems, "real" guards are not given much more psychological preparation or adequate training than this for what is one of the most complex, demanding, and dangerous jobs our society has to offer. They are expected to learn how to adjust to their new employment mostly from on-the-job experience, and from contacts with the "old bulls" during a survival-of-the-fittest orientation period.

* * *

> *The only way you really get to know San Quentin is through experience and time. Some of us take more time and must go through more experiences than others to accomplish this; some really never do get there.*
>
> ORIENTATION MANUAL FOR CORRECTIONAL PERSONNEL AT SAN QUENTIN PRISON
> (July, 1970)

The symbolic interaction between guards and prisoners requires each to play his own role while also forcing the others to play their roles appropriately. *You can not be a prisoner if no one will be your guard, and you can not be a prison guard if no one takes you or your prison seriously.* Therefore, over time a perverted symbiotic relationship developed. As the guards became more aggressive, prisoners became more passive; assertion by the guards led to dependency in the prisoners; self-aggrandizement was met with self-deprecation, authority with helplessness, and the counterpart of the guards' sense of mastery and control was the depression and hopelessness witnessed in the prisoners. As these differences in behavior, mood and perception became more evident to all, the need for the now "righteously" powerful guards to rule the obviously inferior and powerless inmates became a sufficient reason to support almost any further indignity of man against man.

GUARD K: During the inspection, I went to cell 2 to mess up a bed which the prisoner had made and he grabbed me, screaming that he had just made it, and he wasn't going to let me mess it up. He grabbed my throat, and although he was laughing I was pretty scared . . . I lashed out with my stick and hit him in the chin (although not very hard) and when I freed myself I became angry. I wanted to get back in the cell and have a go with him, since he attacked me when I was not ready.

GUARD M: I was surprised at myself . . . I made them call each other names and clean the toilets out with their bare hands. I practically considered the prisoners cattle, and I kept thinking I have to watch out for them in case they try something.

GUARD A: I was tired of seeing the prisoners in their rags and smelling the strong odors of their bodies that filled the cells. I watched them tear at each other on orders given by us. They didn't see it as an experiment. It was real and they were fighting to keep their identity. But we were always there to show them who was boss.

* * *

Power takes as ingratitude the writhing of its victims.

RABINDRANATH TAGORE, *Stray Birds*

Because the first day passed without incident, we were surprised and totally unprepared for the rebellion which broke out on the morning of the second day. The prisoners removed their stocking caps, ripped off their numbers, and barricaded themselves inside the cells by putting their beds against the door. And now the problem was, what were we going to do about this rebellion? The guards were very much upset because the prisoners also began to taunt and curse them to their faces. When the morning shift of guards came on, they were upset at the night shift who, they felt, must have been too permissive and too lenient or else this rebellion would not have taken place. The guards had to handle the rebellion themselves, and what they did was startling to behold.

At first they insisted that reinforcements be called in. The two guards who were waiting on stand-by call at home came in and the night shift of guards voluntarily remained on duty (without extra pay) to bolster the morning shift. The guards met and decided to treat force with force. They got a fire extinguisher which shot a stream of skin-chilling carbon dioxide and forced the prisoners away from the doors, they broke into each cell, stripped the prisoners naked, took the beds out, forced some of the prisoners who were then the ringleaders into solitary confinement, and generally began to harass and intimidate the prisoners.

After crushing the riot, the guards then decided to head off further ones by creating a privileged cell for those who were "good prisoners," then without explanation switching some of the troublemakers into it and some of the good ones out into the other cells. The prisoner ringleaders could not trust these new cellmates because they had not joined in the riot and might even be "snitches." The prisoners never again acted in unity against the system. One of the leaders of the prisoner revolt later confided:

If we had gotten together then, I think we could have taken over the place. But when I saw the revolt wasn't working, I decided to toe the line. Everyone settled into the same pattern. From then on, we were really controlled by the guards.

It was after this episode that the guards really began to demonstrate their inventiveness in the application of arbitrary power. They made the prisoners obey petty, meaningless and often inconsistent rules, forced them to engage in tedious, useless work such as moving cartons back and forth between closets and picking thorns out of their blankets for hours on end. Not only did the prisoners have to sing songs or laugh or refrain from smiling on command, but they were also encouraged to curse and vilify each other publicly during some of the counts. They sounded off their numbers endlessly, and were repeatedly made to do pushups, on occasion with a guard stepping on them or a prisoner sitting on them.

Slowly the prisoners became resigned to their fate and even behaved in ways which actually helped to justify their dehumanizing treatment at the hands of the guards. Analysis of the tape-recorded private conversations between prisoners and of remarks made by them to interviewers revealed that eighty-five percent of the evaluative statements by prisoners about their fellow prisoners, were uncomplimentary and deprecating.

Prisoner: That 2093, "Sarge," the rest of us use him as a scapegoat . . . we couldn't understand how he could mentally comply with everything asked of him.

This result should be taken in the context of an even more surprising one. What do you imagine the prisoners talked about when they were alone in their cells with each other, given a temporary respite from the continual harassment and surveillance by the guards? Girlfriends, career plans, hobbies, politics, etc., were what we assumed would be the major topics of conversation. Not so. Their concerns were almost exclusively riveted to prison topics. Their monitored conversations revealed that only ten percent of the time was devoted to "outside" topics. During the remaining ninety percent of the time they discussed such topics as escape plans, the awful food, grievances, or ingratiation tactics to use with specific guards. The prisoners' obsession with immediate survival concerns made talk about their past and future an idle luxury. But this exclusive focus on prison topics had a doubly negative effect upon the prisoners' adjustment. First, by voluntarily allowing prison topics to occupy their thoughts even when they did not have to continue playing their roles, the prisoners themselves extended the oppressiveness and reality of the experience. Secondly, since the prisoners were all strangers to each other to begin with, they could only know what the others were really like by sharing past experiences and future expectations and observing how they behaved. But what each prisoner observed was his fellow prisoners allowing the guards to humiliate them, acting like compliant sheep, carrying out mindless orders with total obedience, and even being cursed by their fellow prisoners (at a guard's command). After days of living confined together in this tight environment, many of the prisoners did not even know the names of most of the others, where they came from, nor had even the most basic information about what they were like when they were not "prisoners." Under such circumstances, how could a prisoner have respect for his fellows, or any self-respect for what *he* obviously was becoming in the eyes of all those evaluating him?

* * *

> *Life is the art of being well deceived; and in order that the deception may succeed it must be habitual and uninterrupted.*
>
> WM. HAZLITT, "ON PEDANTRY," *The Round Table.*

Thus, the combination of realistic and symbolic elements in this experiment fused to create a vivid illusion of imprisonment. This illusion merged inextricably with reality for at least some of the time for every individual in the situation. It was remarkable how readily we all slipped into our roles, temporarily gave up our identities, and allowed these assigned roles and the social forces in the situation to guide, shape and eventually to control our freedom of thought and action.

Can it really be, you wonder, that intelligent, educated volunteers could have lost sight of the reality that they were merely acting a part in an elaborate game (of cops and robbers) which would eventually end? There are many available sources of evidence indicating not only that they did, but also, so did we and so did other apparently sensible, responsible adults. A few examples will convey the extent to which a role-playing simulation experience can, under certain circumstances, become a totally involving life situation.

Prisoner 819, who had gone into a rage followed by an uncontrollable crying fit, was about to be prematurely released from the prison when a guard lined up the prisoners and had them chant in unison, "819 is a bad prisoner. Because of what 819 did to prison property we all must suffer. 819 is a bad prisoner," over and over again. When we realized 819 might be overhearing this, we rushed into the room where 819 was supposed to be resting, only to find him in tears, prepared to go back into that prison because he could not leave as long as the others thought he was a "bad prisoner." Sick as he felt, he had to prove to them he was not a "bad" prisoner. He had to be persuaded that he was not a prisoner at all, that the others were also just students, that this was just an experiment and not a prison and the prison staff were only research psychologists.

Consider our overreaction to the rumor of a mass escape plot which one of the guards allegedly overheard. It went as follows: Prisoner 8612, previously released for emotional disturbance, was only faking. He was going to round up a bunch of his friends and they would storm the prison right after visiting hours. Instead of collecting data on the pattern of rumor transmission, we made plans to maintain the security of our institution. After putting a confederate informer into the cell 8612 had occupied to get specific information about the escape plans, the Superintendent went back to the Palo Alto Police Department to request transfer of our prisoners to the old city jail. This impassioned plea was turned down at the last minute when the problem of insurance and city liability for our prisoners was raised by a city official. Angered at this lack of institutional cooperation, the staff formulated another plan. Our jail was dismantled, the prisoners, chained and blindfolded, were carted off to a remote storage room. When the conspirators arrived, they would be told the study was over, their friends had been sent home, there was nothing left to liberate. After they left, we would redouble the security features of our prison, making any future escape attempts futile. We even planned to lure ex-prisoner 8612 back on some pretext and then imprison him because he had been released on false pretenses! The rumor turned out to be just that—a full day had passed in which we collected little or no data, worked incredibly hard to tear down and then rebuild our prison. Our reaction however, was as much one of relief and joy as of exhaustion and frustration.

Perhaps the most telling account of the insidious development of this new reality, of the gradual Kafkaesque metamorphosis of good into evil, is evident in excerpts from the diary of one of the guards, Guard A:

PRIOR TO START OF EXPERIMENT: As I am a pacifist and nonaggressive individual. I cannot see a time when I might guard and/or maltreat other living things.

AFTER ORIENTATION MEETING: Buying uniforms at the end of the meeting confirms the game-like atmosphere of this thing. I doubt whether many of us share the expectations of "seriousness" that the experimenters seem to have.

FIRST DAY: Feel sure that the prisoners will make fun of my appearance and evolve my first basic strategy—mainly not to smile at anything they say or do which would be admitting it's all only a game. . . . At cell 3 I stop and setting my voice hard and low say to #5486, "what are you smiling at?" "Nothing, Mr. Correctional Officer." "Well see that you don't." (As I walk off I feel stupid.)

SECOND DAY: 5704 asked for a cigarette and I ignored him—because I am a non-smoker and could not empathize. . . . Meanwhile since I was feeling empathetic towards 1037, I determined not to talk with him . . . after we had Count and lights out [Guard D] and I held a loud conversation about going home to our girlfriends and what we were going to do to them.

THIRD DAY: (Preparing for the first Visitors' Night.) After warning the prisoners not to make any complaints unless they wanted the visit terminated fast, we finally brought in the first parents. I made sure I was one of the guards on the yard, because this was my first chance for the type of manipulative power that I really like—being a very noticed figure with almost complete control over what is said or not. While the parents and prisoners sat in chairs, I sat on the end of the table dangling my feet and contradicting anything I felt like. This was the first part of the experiment I was really enjoying. . . . 817 is being obnoxious and bears watching.

FOURTH DAY: . . . The psychologist rebukes me for handcuffing and blindfolding a prisoner before leaving the [counseling] office, and I resentfully reply that it is both necessary security and my business anyway.

FIFTH DAY: I harass "Sarge" who continues to stubbornly overrespond to all commands. I have singled him out for special abuse both because he begs for it and because I simply don't like him. The real trouble starts at dinner. The new prisoner (416) refuses to eat his sausage . . . we throw him into the Hole ordering him to hold sausages in each hand. We have a crisis of authority, this rebellious conduct potentially undermines the complete control we have over the others. We decide to play upon prisoner solidarity and tell the new one that all the others will be deprived of visitors if he does not eat his dinner. . . . I walk by and slam my stick into the Hole door . . . I am very angry at this prisoner for causing discomfort and trouble for the others. I decided to force feed him, but he wouldn't eat. I let the food slide down his face. I didn't believe it was me doing it. I hated myself for making him eat but I hated him more for not eating.

SIXTH DAY: The experiment is over. I feel elated but am shocked to find some other guards disappointed somewhat because of the loss of money and some because they are enjoying themselves.

We were no longer dealing with an intellectual exercise in which an hypothesis was being evaluated in the dispassionate manner dictated by the canons of the scientific method. We were caught up in the passion of the present, the suffering, the need to control people not variables, the escalation of power and all of the unexpected things which were erupting around and within us. We had to end this experiment! So our planned two-week simulation was aborted after only six (was it only six?) days and nights.

* * *

We've travelled too far, and our momentum has
taken over; we move idly towards eternity,
without possibility of reprieve or hope of explanation.

TOM STOPPARD,
Rosencrantz and Guildenstein Are Dead

But was it worth all the suffering just to prove what everyone knows, that some people are sadistic, others weak and prisons are not a bed of roses? If that is all we demonstrated in this research then it was certainly not worth the anguish. We believe there are many significant implications to be derived from this experience, only a few of which can be suggested here.

The potential social value of this study derives precisely from the fact that normal, healthy, educated young men could be so radically transformed under the institutional pressures of a "prison environment." The argument runs, if this could happen in so short a time, without the excesses that are possible in real prisons, in the "cream-of-the-crop" of American youth, then one can only shudder at imagining what society is doing both to the actual guards and prisoners who are at this very moment participating in that unnatural "social experiment."

The pathology observed in this study cannot be reasonably attributed to preexisting personality differences of the subjects, that option being eliminated by our selection procedures, and random assignment. Rather, the subjects' abnormal social and personal reactions are best seen as a product of their *transaction* with an environment whose values and contingencies supported the production of behavior which would be pathological in other settings, but were "appropriate" in this prison. Had we observed comparable reactions in a real prison, the psychiatrist undoubtedly would have been able to attribute any prisoner's behavior to character defects or personality maladjustment, while critics of the prison system would have been as quick to label the guards as "psychopathic." This tendency to locate the source of behavior disorders *inside* a particular person or group underestimates the power of situational forces to control behavior while overestimating the efficacy of personality or trait dispositions. A substantial body of research indicates that there is little transsituational generality of personality traits and further, that personality consistency is more in the minds of observers than in the behavior of those observed.

Unfortunately, the insistence by traditional psychiatrists, psychoanalysts and personality psychologists that socially deviant or pathological behavior is the product of weak egos, latent traits and a host of other assumed inner dispositions has done a great disservice to mankind. Those in positions of power have been given an arsenal of labels to apply to those without power, the poor, the dissidents, the nonconformists, the revolutionaries, etc., thereby sustaining the status quo by making *people* the problem and not the economic/social/political inequities in their life situation. Moreover, this dispositional analysis becomes a weapon in the hands of reactionary legislators and law enforcers since defective problem people are then "treated" by one of their available institutions while problem situations are ignored or dismissed as irrelevant or too complex to change easily.

* * *

> *Of all the vulgar modes of escaping from the consideration of social and moral influence on the human mind, the most vulgar is that of attributing the diversities of conduct and character to inherent natural differences.*
>
> J. S. MILL, *Principles of Political Economy*

The most disturbing lesson of our research comes from the parallels between what occurred in that basement mock prison and daily experiences in our own lives—and we presume yours. The physical institution of prison is but a concrete and steel metaphor for the existence of more pervasive, albeit less obvious, prisons of the mind which each of us daily creates, populates, and perpetuates. We speak here of the prisons of racism, sexism, despair, shyness, "neurotic hang-ups," and the like. The social convention of marriage, as one example, becomes for many couples a state of imprisonment in which one partner agrees to be prisoner or guard, forcing or allowing the other to play the reciprocal role—invariably without making the contract explicit. To what extent do we allow ourselves to become imprisoned by docilely accepting the roles others assign us or, indeed, choose to remain prisoners because being passive and dependent frees us from the need to act and be responsible for our actions?

Yet, in spite of the profoundly negative characterization of prisons drawn by our results and the reports of others, there is cause for guarded optimism about the possibility of their constructive reform. If, indeed, the pathology of prisons can be isolated as a product of the power relations in the social psychological structure of the institution itself, change is conceivable. Social institutions, being the creations of human beings—our little experiments in social and political control—are susceptible to modification when confronted by a human consciousness protesting their inadequacy and evils, supported by an informed electorate concerned about eliminating all forms of injustice. Institutionalized prisons must be radically changed, alternatives to incarceration must be sought so that human values are promoted and celebrated rather than crushed and perverted—but "it will not be easy."

CONFORMING

Conforming may be regarded as a special case of being molded. It represents a relatively straightforward form of social influence, in which people change their behavior or attitudes so as to be in closer accord with other members of their group, or so as to follow the dictates of some higher authority. But whereas it is relatively straightforward and overt, conformity remains a puzzling and often disconcerting phenomenon because it involves people's subordinating their own judgments and standards to the judgments and standards of others.

People's capacity for "blind conformity" was dramatized in Solomon Asch's classic series of experiments. Unsuspecting subjects found themselves being unanimously disagreed with by a group of fellow students with respect to what seemed to be simple perceptual judgments. In a large percentage of cases, the subjects decided to go along with the group. Of considerable importance was Asch's finding that the presence of just one other student who agreed with the subject's judgments markedly reduced the extent of conformity. The single ally apparently provided the modicum of social support needed to help one maintain his independence in the face of otherwise unanimous repudiation.

Irving Janis's brilliant analysis of "groupthink" among policy makers forcefully documents the power of pressures toward conformity in high-level decision-making groups. Both in President Kennedy's inner circle of policy advisers who gave the go-ahead to the ill-fated Bay of Pigs invasion and in the council who advised President Johnson to escalate the Vietnam war, critical judgment seems to have been suspended in favor of shared illusions. The Watergate tapes released in early 1974 clearly suggested that groupthink reigned in President Nixon's White House as well. Paradoxically, Janis points out, the higher the morale and *esprit de corps* of a planning group, the more likely it may be to suppress dissent and undermine critical thinking.

Conformity of thought and action is especially likely to occur in organizational hierarchies, with subordinates readily acceding to the wishes of their superiors. The massacre at My Lai is but one example of a case in which illegal and immoral actions resulted from a subordinate's decision to "just follow orders." Stanley Milgram worked within the context of another organizational hierarchy—that involving the psychological experimenter and his subjects—to explore the conditions of obedience and disobedience to authority. His results were both enlightening and frightening, for they demonstrated that the power of a "legitimate authority" to elicit destructive behavior was much greater than most observers would have predicted or imagined.

Some degree of conformity is clearly a necessity of social life. We must be responsive to the wishes of others and adhere to common norms and conventions if we are to live in communities and interact meaningfully with our fellow men and women. As we have seen in the two previous sections, each of us makes use of comparisons with and feedback from others in developing our own standards and self-evaluations. As the selections in this section demonstrate, however, this dependence can easily go too far, leading to distorted judgments, bad decisions, and harmful actions. Each of us must walk a tightrope between excessive conformity, on the one hand, and renunciation and withdrawal, on the other. The character of life in society hangs to a large extent on the success with which we walk this tightrope.

Effects of Group Pressure upon the Modification and Distortion of Judgments

Solomon E. Asch

We shall here describe in summary form the conception and first findings of a program of investigation into the conditions of independence and submission to group pressure.

Our immediate object was to study the social and personal conditions that induce individuals to resist or to yield to group pressures when the latter are perceived to be *contrary to fact*. The issues which this problem raises are of obvious consequence for society; it can be of decisive importance whether or not a group will, under certain conditions, submit to existing pressures. Equally direct are the consequences for individuals and our understanding of them, since it is a decisive fact about a person whether he possesses the freedom to act independently, or whether he characteristically submits to group pressures.

Basic to the current approach has been the axiom that group pressures characteristically induce psychological changes *arbitrarily*, in far-reaching disregard of the material properties of the given conditions. This mode of thinking has almost exclusively stressed the slavish submission of individuals to group forces, has neglected to inquire into their possibilities for independence and for productive relations with the human environment, and has virtually denied the capacity of men under certain conditions to rise above group passion and prejudice. It was our aim to contribute to a clarification of these questions, important both for theory and for their human implications, by means of direct observation of the effects of groups upon the decisions and evaluations of individuals.

Abridged from H. Guetzkow (Ed.), *Groups, Leadership, and Men,* Pittsburgh: Carnegie Press, 1951, pp. 177–190, with permission of the author and the publisher.

THE EXPERIMENT AND FIRST RESULTS

To this end we developed an experimental technique which has served as the basis for the present series of studies. A group of eight individuals was instructed to judge a series of simple, clearly structured perceptual relations—to match the length of a given line with one of three unequal lines. Each member of the group announced his judgments publicly. In the midst of this monotonous "test" one individual found himself suddenly contradicted by the entire group, and this contradiction was repeated again and again in the course of the experiment. The group in question had, with the exception of one member, previously met with the experimenter and received instructions to respond at certain points with wrong—and unanimous—judgments. The errors of the majority were large (ranging between ½" and 1¾") and of an order not encountered under control conditions. The outstanding person—the critical subject—whom we had placed in the position of a *minority of one* in the midst of a *unanimous majority*—was the object of investigation. He faced, possibly for the first time in his life, a situation in which a group unanimously contradicted the evidence of his senses.

This procedure was the starting point of the investigation and the point of departure for the study of further problems. Its main features were the following: (1) The critical subject was submitted to two contradictory and irreconcilable forces—the evidence of his own experience of a clearly perceived relation, and the unanimous evidence of a group of equals. (2) Both forces were part of the immediate situation; the majority was concretely present, surrounding the subject physically. (3) The critical subject, who was requested together with all others to state his judgments publicly, was obliged to declare himself and to take a definite stand *vis-à-vis* the group. (4) The situation possessed a self-contained character. The critical subject could not avoid or evade the dilemma by reference to conditions external to the experimental situation. (It may be mentioned at this point that the forces generated by the given conditions acted so quickly upon the critical subjects that instances of suspicion were infrequent.)

The technique employed permitted a simple quantitative measure of the "majority effect" in terms of the frequency of errors in the direction of the distorted estimates of the majority. At the same time we were concerned to obtain evidence of the ways in which the subjects perceived the group, to establish whether they became doubtful, whether they were tempted to join the majority. Most important, it was our object to establish the grounds of the subject's independence or yielding—whether, for example, the yielding subject was aware of the effect of the majority upon him, whether he abandoned his judgment deliberately or compulsively. To this end we constructed a comprehensive set of questions which served as the basis of an individual interview immediately following the experimental period. Toward the conclusion of the interview each subject was informed fully of the purpose of the experiment, of his role and of that of the majority.

Both the members of the majority and the critical subjects were male college students. We shall report the results for a total of fifty critical subjects in this experiment. On certain trials the majority of group members responded correctly; these were the "neutral" trials. There were twelve critical trials on which the majority responded incorrectly.

The quantitative results are clear and unambiguous.

1. There was a marked movement toward the majority. One third of all the estimates on the critical trials were errors identical with or in the direction of the distorted estimates of the majority. The significance of this finding becomes clear in the light of the virtual absence of errors in the control group, in which subjects recorded their estimates in writing.
2. At the same time the effect of the majority was far from complete. The preponderance of estimates in the critical group (68 percent) was correct despite the pressure of the majority.
3. We found evidence of extreme individual differences. There were in the critical group subjects who remained independent without exception, and there were those who went nearly all the time with the majority. (The maximum possible number of errors was 12, while the actual range of errors was 0–11.) One fourth of the critical subjects were completely independent; at the other extreme, one third of the group displaced the estimates toward the majority in one half or more of the trials.

The differences between the critical subjects in their reactions to the given conditions were equally striking. There were subjects who remained completely confident throughout. At the other extreme were those who became disoriented, doubt-ridden, and experienced a powerful impulse not to appear different from the majority.

For purposes of illustration we include a brief description of one independent and one yielding subject.

INDEPENDENT

After a few trials he appeared puzzled, hesitant. He announced all disagreeing answers in the form of "Three, sir; two, sir"; not so with the unanimous answers on the neutral trials. At Trial 4 he answered immediately after the first member of the group, shook his head, blinked, and whispered to his neighbor: "Can't help it, that's one." His later answers came in a whispered voice, accompanied by a deprecating smile. At one point he grinned embarrassedly, and whispered explosively to his neighbor: "I always disagree—darn it!" During the questioning, this subject's constant refrain was: "I called them as I saw them, sir." He insisted that his estimates were right without, however, committing himself as to whether the others were wrong, remarking that "that's the way I see them and that's the way they see them." If he had to make a practical decision under similar circumstances, he declared, "I would follow my own view, though part of my reason would tell me that I might be wrong." Immediately following the experiment the majority engaged this subject in a brief discussion. When they pressed him to say whether the entire group was wrong and he alone right, he turned upon them defiantly, exclaiming: "You're *probably* right, but you *may* be wrong!" To the disclosure of the experiment this subject reacted with the statement that he felt "exultant and relieved," adding, "I do not deny that at times I had the feeling: 'to heck with it, I'll go along with the rest.'"

YIELDING

This subject went with the majority in 11 out of 12 trials. He appeared nervous and somewhat confused, but he did not attempt to evade discussion; on the contrary, he was helpful and tried to answer to the best of his ability. He opened the discussion with the statement: "If I'd been first I probably would have responded differently"; this was his way of stating that he had adopted the majority estimates. The primary factor in his case was loss of confidence. He perceived the majority as a decided group, acting without hesitation: "If they had been doubtful I probably would have changed, but they answered with such confidence." Certain of his errors, he explained, were due to the doubtful nature of the comparisons; in such instances he went with the majority. When the object of the experiment was explained, the subject volunteered: "I suspected about the middle—but tried to push it out of my mind." It is of interest that his suspicion did not restore his confidence or diminish the power of the majority. Equally striking is his report that he assumed the experiment to involve an "illusion" to which the others, but not he, were subject. This assumption too did not help to free him; on the contrary, he acted as if his divergence from the majority was a sign of defect. The principal impression this subject produced was of one so caught up by immediate difficulties that he lost clear reasons for his actions, and could make no reasonable decisions.

A FIRST ANALYSIS OF INDIVIDUAL DIFFERENCES

On the basis of the interview data described earlier, we undertook to differentiate and describe the major forms of reaction to the experimental situation, which we shall now briefly summarize.

Among the *independent* subjects we distinguished the following main categories:

1. Independence based on *confidence* in one's perception and experience. The most striking characteristic of these subjects is the vigor with which they withstand the group opposition. Though they are sensitive to the group, and experience the conflict, they show a resilience in coping with it, which is expressed in their continuing reliance on their perception and the effectiveness with which they shake off the oppressive group opposition.

2. Quite different are those subjects who are independent and *withdrawn*. These do not react in a spontaneously emotional way, but rather on the basis of explicit principles concerning the necessity of being an individual.

3. A third group of independent subjects manifests considerable tension and *doubt,* but adhere to their judgment on the basis of a felt necessity to deal adequately with the task.

The following were the main categories of reaction among the *yielding* subjects, or those who went with the majority during one half or more of the trials.

1. *Distortion of perception* under the stress of group pressure. In this category belong a very few subjects who yield completely, but are not aware that their estimates have been displaced or distorted by the majority. These subjects report that they came to perceive the majority estimates as correct.

2. *Distortion of judgment.* Most submitting subjects belong to this category. The factor of greatest importance in this group is a decision the subjects reach that their perceptions are inaccurate, and that those of the majority are correct. These subjects suffer from primary doubt and lack of confidence; on this basis they feel a strong tendency to join the majority.

3. *Distortion of action.* The subjects in this group do not suffer a modification of perception nor do they conclude that they are wrong. They yield because of an overmastering need not to appear different from or inferior to others, because of an inability to tolerate the appearance of defectiveness in the eyes of the group. These subjects suppress their observations and voice the majority position with awareness of what they are doing.

The results are sufficient to establish that independence and yielding are not psychologically homogeneous, that submission to group pressure and freedom from pressure can be the result of different psychological conditions.

THE EFFECT OF NONUNANIMOUS MAJORITIES

Evidence obtained from the basic experiment suggested that the condition of being exposed *alone* to the opposition of a "compact majority" may have played a decisive role in determining the course and strength of the effects observed. Accordingly we undertook to investigate in a series of successive variations the effects of *nonunanimous* majorities. The technical problem of altering the uniformity of a majority is, in terms of our procedure, relatively simple. The following were some of the variations employed:

1. *The presence of a "true partner."* (*a*) In the midst of the majority were *two* naïve, critical subjects. The subjects were separated spatially, being seated in the fourth and eighth positions, respectively. Each therefore heard his judgments confirmed by one other person (provided the other person remained independent), one prior to, the other after announcing his own judgment. In addition, each experienced a break in the unanimity of the majority. (*b*) In a further variation the "partner" to the critical subject was a member of the group who had been instructed to respond correctly throughout. This procedure permits the exact control of the partner's responses. The partner was always seated in the fourth position; he therefore announced his estimates in each case before the critical subject.

The results clearly demonstrate that a disturbance of the unanimity of the majority markedly increased the independence of the critical subjects. The frequency of promajority errors dropped to 10.4 percent of the total number of estimates in variation (*a*), and to 5.5 percent in variation (*b*). These results are to be compared with the frequency of yielding to the unanimous majorities in the basic experiment, which was 32 percent of the total number of estimates. It is clear that the presence in the field of *one other* individual who responded correctly was sufficient to deplete the power of the majority, and in some cases to destroy it. This finding is all the more striking in the light of other variations which demonstrate the effect of even small minorities provided they are unanimous. Indeed, we have been able to show that a unanimous majority of 3 is, under the given conditions, far more effective than a majority of 8 containing 1 dissenter. That critical subjects will under these conditions free themselves of a majority of 7 and join forces with one other person in the minority is, we believe, a result significant for theory. It points to a fundamental psychological difference between the condition of being alone and having a minimum of human support.

2. *Withdrawal of a "true partner."* What will be the effect of providing the critical subject with a partner who responds correctly and then withdrawing him? The critical subject started with a partner who responded correctly. The partner was a member of the majority who had been instructed to respond correctly and to "desert" to the majority in the middle of the experiment. This procedure permits the observation of the same subject in the course of the transition from one condition to another. The withdrawal of the partner produced a powerful and unexpected result. We had assumed that the critical subject, having gone through the experience of opposing the majority with a minimum of support, would maintain his independence when alone. Contrary to this expectation, we found that the experience of having had and then lost a partner restored the majority effect to its full force, the proportion of errors rising to 28.5 percent of all judgments, in contrast to the preceding level of 5.5 percent. Further experimentation is needed to establish whether the critical subjects were responding to the sheer fact of being alone, or to the fact that the partner abandoned them.

THE ROLE OF MAJORITY SIZE

To gain further understanding of the majority effect, we varied the size of the majority in several different variations. The majorities, which were in each case unanimous, consisted of 2, 3, 4, 8, and 10–15 persons, respectively. In addition, we studied the limiting case in which the critical subject was opposed by one instructed subject.

With the opposition reduced to 1, the majority effect all but disappeared. When the opposition proceeded from a group of 2, it produced a measurable though small distortion, the errors being 12.8 percent of the total number of estimates. The effect appeared in full force with a majority of 3. Larger majorities did not produce effects greater than a majority of 3.

The effect of a majority is often silent, revealing little of its operation to the subject, and often hiding it from the experimenter. To examine the range of effects it is capable of inducing, decisive variations of conditions are necessary. An indication of one effect is furnished by the following variation in which the conditions of the basic experiment were simply reversed. Here the majority, consisting of a group of 16, was naïve; in the midst of it we placed a single individual who responded wrongly according to instructions. Under these conditions the members of the naïve majority reacted to the lone dissenter with amusement. Contagious laughter spread through the group at the droll minority of 1. Of significance is the fact that the members lacked awareness that they drew their strength from the majority, and that their reactions would change radically if they faced the dissenter individually. These observations demonstrate the role of social support as a source of power and stability, in contrast to the preceding investigations which stressed the effects of social opposition. Both aspects must be explicitly considered in a unified formulation of the effects of group conditions on the formation and change of judgments.

* * *

For a full account of this research, see S. E. Asch, "Studies of independence and submission to group pressure: I. A minority of one against a unanimous majority," *Psychological Monographs*, 1956, *70*.

Groupthink among Policy Makers

Irving L. Janis

I have been studying a series of notorious decisions made by government leaders, including major fiascos such as the Vietnam escalation decisions of the Lyndon B. Johnson administration, the Bay of Pigs invasion plan of the John F. Kennedy administration, and the Korean Crisis decision of the Harry Truman administration, which unintentionally provoked Red China to enter the war. In addition, I have examined some fiascos by European governments, such as the policy of appeasement carried out by Neville Chamberlain and his inner cabinet during the late 1930s—a policy which turned over to the Nazis the populations and military resources of Austria, Czechoslovakia, and other small countries of Europe. In all these instances, the decision-making groups took little account of some of the major consequences of their actions, including the moral and humanitarian implications.

When we examine how each of these decisions was made we find that it was rarely the work of just one man—even though historians may refer to it as the President's or the Prime Minister's decision. Rather, the decision was a group product, resulting from a series of meetings of a small body of government officials and advisers who constituted a cohesive group of policy makers. For example, when we look into the way the Vietnam policies of the Johnson administration were arrived at, we discover very quickly that the key decisions were made by a small cohesive group. In addition to the President, the group included McGeorge Bundy, the special White House assistant (later replaced by Walt Rostow); William Moyers, press secretary (later replaced by George Christian); Robert McNamara, secretary of defense (replaced during the last months of the Johnson administration by Clark Clifford); and Dean Rusk, secretary of state (who managed to remain in Johnson's policy-making group from the

Abridged from N. Sanford, C. Comstock, et al., *Sanctions for Evil,* San Francisco: Jossey-Bass, 1971, pp. 71–89, with permission of the author and the publisher.

bitter beginning to the bitter end). For several years George Ball, who was undersecretary of state, also participated in the meetings. The group also included Earle Wheeler, chairman of the Joint Chiefs of Staff, and Richard Helms, director of the Central Intelligence Agency.

It was surprising for me to discover the extent to which this group and other such small groups of policy makers displayed the phenomena of social conformity regularly encountered in studies of group dynamics among ordinary citizens. For example, some of the phenomena appear to be completely in line with findings from social psychological experiments showing that powerful social pressures are brought to bear by the members of a cohesive group when a dissident begins to voice his objections to a group consensus. Other phenomena I describe are reminiscent of the shared illusions observed in encounter groups and friendship cliques when the members simultaneously reach a peak of group-y feelings. Above all, numerous indications point to the development of group norms that bolster morale at the expense of critical thinking.

To begin, I mention here the main sources for the Vietnam case study. One is an insightful article by James C. Thomson, Jr.,[1] a historian at Harvard, who spent many years as a participant observer in the government, first in the State Department and then in the White House as an assistant to Bundy. Another is a book by David Kraslow and Stuart H. Loory,[2] two journalists who interviewed many government officials involved in forming policies concerning the Vietnam war. The third is a book by Townsend Hoopes,[3] who was acting secretary of the air force in the Cabinet. Hoopes's book is especially valuable for understanding the social and political pressures put on McNamara, Clifford, and other high officials who, toward the end of the Johnson administration, became disillusioned and began to favor deescalation of the war. Using these and several other references, we can get some idea of the forces that enabled intelligent, conscientious policy makers to make the series of grossly miscalculated decisions that had such destructive effects on the people of Vietnam and such corrosive effects within our country.

One of the first things we learn from these accounts is that when the in-group of key advisers met with Johnson every Tuesday (they sometimes called themselves the Tuesday Luncheon Group), their meetings were characterized by a games theory detachment concerning the consequences of the war policies they were discussing. The members of this group adopted a special vocabulary for describing the Vietnam war, using terms such as body counts, armed reconnaissance, and surgical strikes, which they picked up from their military colleagues. The Vietnam policy mak-

1 J. Thomson, "How could Vietnam happen? An autopsy," *The Atlantic,* April 1968, pp. 47–53.

2 D. Kraslow and S. Loory, *The Secret Search for Peace in Vietnam* (New York: Vintage, 1968).

3 T. Hoopes, *The Limits of Intervention* (New York: McKay, 1969).

ers, by using this professional military vocabulary, were able to avoid in their discussions with each other all direct references to human suffering and thus to form an attitude of detachment similar to that of surgeons. But although an attitude of detachment may have functional value for those who must execute distressing operations, it makes it all too easy for policy makers to dehumanize the victims of war and to resort to destructive military solutions without considering their human consequences.

Thomson, who has reported this tendency from close at hand, recounts a memorable meeting in late 1964 when the policy planners were discussing how much bombing and strafing should be carried out against Vietnamese villages. The issue was resolved when an assistant secretary of state spoke up saying, "It seems to me that our orchestration in this instance ought to be mainly violins, but with periodic touches here and there of brass." Thomson, in retrospect, came to realize that he had himself undergone attitude changes, that he had acquired the same sense of aloof detachment that pervaded the war policy discussions of Washington bureaucrats. Back at Harvard, after leaving his post in the White House, he was shocked to realize that the young men in front of him in the classroom were the human beings in the manpower pool he had been talking about so detachedly when discussing problems of increasing the number of draftees with the policy makers in Washington.

This dehumanization tendency is closely related to another characteristic of Johnson's policy-making group: reliance on shared stereotypes of the enemy and of the peoples of Asia. Their grossly oversimplified views overlooked the vast differences in political orientation, historic traditions, and cultural patterns among the nations of Asia. Their sloganistic thinking about the North Vietnam Communists overlooked powerful nationalistic strivings, particularly North Vietnam efforts to ward off Chinese domination. As a historian, Thomson was shocked to realize the extent to which crudely propagandistic conceptions entered into the group's plans and policies. The policy makers, according to Thomson, were disposed to take a very hard-nosed, military stance partly because of these stereotyped notions. The dominant view demonized the enemy as embodying all evils, which legitimized the use of relentlessly destructive means. These stereotypes were evidently incorporated into the norms of the policy-making group, so it was very difficult for any member to introduce a more sophisticated viewpoint.

In a cohesive group that adopts such norms, what happens when a member starts expressing his mild doubts and says, "Let's sit back for a moment and think this over; don't we need to make some distinctions here?" or "Shouldn't we talk about some of the consequences we may have overlooked?" Such questions must often go through the minds of the participants before they agree on a policy that has some obvious drawbacks. But as soon as anybody starts to speak about his doubts, he discovers, often in subtle ways, that the others are becoming somewhat irritated and that he is in the presence of powerful group pressures to be a booster, not a detractor.

Typically, a cohesive group, like the in-group of policy makers in the Johnson administration, develops a set of norms requiring loyal support of past decisions. Each member is under strong pressure to maintain his commitment to the group's decisions and to support unquestionably the arguments and justifications they have worked out together to explain away obvious errors in their judgment. Given this shared commitment, the members put pressure on each other to continue marching to the same old drum beat and to insist that sooner or later everyone will be in step with it. They become inhibited about expressing doubts to insiders as well as outsiders with regard to the ultimate success and morality of their policies.

Whenever a group develops a strong "we feeling" and manifests a high degree of solidarity, there are powerful internal as well as external pressures to conform to the group's norms. A member of an executive in-group may feel constrained to tone down his criticisms, to present only those arguments that will be readily tolerated by the others, and to remain silent about objections that the others might regard as being beyond the pale. We can surmise from studies of work teams, social clubs, and informal friendship groups that such constraints arise at least partly because each member comes to rely upon the group to provide him with emotional support for coping with the stresses of decision-making. When facing any important decision, especially during a serious crisis, a group member often develops feelings of insecurity or anxiety about risks that could adversely affect the interests of the nation or organization and that could damage his own career. Moreover, most policy decisions generate conflicts between different standards of conduct, between ethical ideas and humanitarian values on the one hand and the utilitarian demands of national or organizational goals, practical politics, and economics on the other. A platitudinous policy maker is likely to reassure his colleagues by reminding them that you can't make an omelet without breaking some eggs. Nevertheless, each man's awareness that moral and ethical values are being sacrificed in order to arrive at a viable policy can give rise to distressing feelings of shame, guilt, depression, and related emotional reactions associated with lowering of self-esteem. Given all the uncertainties and dilemmas that arise whenever one shares in the responsibility of making a vital decision, such as war policies affecting the welfare and survival of entire nations, it is understandable that the members of a decision-making body should strive to alleviate stress.

Some individuals in public office are extraordinarily self-confident and may not need the support of a cohesive group when their decisions are subject to public criticism. I think, for example, of the spirited symphony orchestra conductor Thomas Beecham, who once said, "I have made just one mistake in my entire life and that was one time when I thought

I was wrong but actually I was right." Not everybody who is accustomed to putting it on the line as a decision maker is able to maintain such unassailable self-confidence, however. So, not surprisingly, most members of a cohesive policy-making group strive to develop a sense of unanimity and esprit de corps that help them to maintain their morale by reaffirming the positive value of the policies to which they are committed. And, just as in friendship cliques, they regard any deviant within the group who insists on calling attention to the defects of the policies as objectionable and disloyal.

Social psychologists have observed this tendency in studies of students' clubs and other small groups. Whenever a member says something out of line with group norms, the other members increase communication with the deviant. Attempts to influence the nonconformist member to revise or to tone down his dissident ideas continue as long as most members of the group feel reasonably hopeful about talking him into changing his mind. But if they fail after repeated attempts, the amount of communication they direct toward the deviant goes down markedly. From then on, the members begin to exclude him, often quite subtly at first and later more obviously, to restore the unity of the group. A social psychological experiment conducted by Stanley Schachter in America and replicated in seven different European countries showed that the more cohesive the group and the more relevant the issue to the goals of the group, the greater the inclination of the members to reject a recalcitrant deviant.

During Johnson's administration, when any member of the in-group began to express doubts—as some of them certainly did—they were treated in a rather standardized way that strongly resembled the research findings just described. At first, the dissenter was made to feel at home—provided that he lived up to two restrictions: that he did not voice his doubts to outsiders, which would play into the hands of the opposition; and that he kept the criticisms within the bounds of acceptable deviation, not challenging any of the fundamental assumptions that went into the prior commitments the group had made. Thomson refers to such doubters as domesticated dissenters. One domesticated dissenter was Moyers, who was described as Johnson's closest adviser. When Moyers arrived at a meeting, we are told, the President greeted him with, "Well, here comes Mr. Stop-the-Bombing." But Moyers and the other domesticated dissenters, like Ball, did not stay domesticated forever. These men appear to have become casualties of subsequent group pressures; they resigned long before the entire Johnson administration became a casualty of the Vietnam war policy, long before that startling day when Johnson appeared on television and tearfully explained why he was not going to run again.

Given the series of cautionary examples and the constant reaffirmation of norms, every dissenter is likely to feel under strong pressure to suppress his doubts, misgivings, and objections. The main norm, as I have already suggested, becomes that of sticking with the policies on which the group has already concurred, even if those policies are working out badly and have some horrible consequences that may disturb the conscience of every member. The main criterion used to judge the morality as well as the practical efficacy of the policy is group concurrence. The belief that "we are a wise and good group" extends to any decision the group makes: "Since we are a good group," the members feel, "anything we decide to do must be good."

In a sense, loyalty to the policy-making group becomes the highest form of morality for the members. That loyalty requires them to avoid raising critical issues, to avoid calling a halt to soft-headed thinking, and to avoid questioning weak arguments, even when the individual member begins to have doubts and to wonder whether they are indeed behaving in a soft-headed manner. This loyalty is one of the key characteristics of what I call groupthink.

I use the term *groupthink* as a quick and easy way to refer to a mode of thinking that people engage in when they are deeply involved in a cohesive in-group, when concurrence-seeking becomes so dominant that it tends to override critical thinking. *Groupthink* is a term of the same order as the words in the newspeak vocabulary George Orwell presents in his dismaying world of *1984,* where we find terms like *doublethink* and *crimethink.* In putting groupthink into that Orwellian class of words, I realize that it takes on an invidious connotation. Exactly such a connotation is intended since the term refers to a decline in mental efficiency and in the ability to test reality and to make moral judgments. Most of the main symptoms of groupthink arise because the members of decision-making groups avoid being too harsh in their judgments of their leader's or their colleagues' ideas. They adopt a soft line of criticism, even in their own thinking. At their meetings, all the members are amiable and seek complete concurrence on every important issue, with no bickering or conflict to spoil the cozy atmosphere.

Paradoxically, however, soft-headed groups can be extraordinarily hard hearted when it comes to dealing with out-groups or enemies. In dealing with a rival nation, policy makers in an amiable group atmosphere find it relatively easy to resort to dehumanizing solutions, such as authorizing large-scale bombing attacks on large numbers of harmless civilians in the noble cause of persuading an unfriendly government to negotiate at the peace table. An affable group of government officials is unlikely to pursue the ticklish, difficult, and controversial issues that arise when alternatives to a harsh military solution come up for discussion. Nor is there much patience for those members who call attention to moral issues, who imply that this "fine group of ours, with its humanitarianism and its high-minded principles," may be capable of adopting a course of action that is inhumane and immoral. Such cohesive groups also tend to resist new information that contradicts the shared judgments of the members. Anyone, no matter how central a member of the group, who contradicts the consensus that has already started to emerge is regarded as a deviant threatening the unity of the group.

Many other sources of human error, of course, can impair the quality of policy decisions. Some errors stem from psychological factors in the personalities of the decision makers. Also, special circumstances can create undue fatigue and other stresses that interfere with adequate decision-making. In addition, numerous institutional factors embedded in the social structure may make for inefficiency and may prevent adequate communication from knowledgeable experts. The concept of groupthink puts the finger on a source of trouble that resides neither in the single individual (as when a man's judgments suffer from his prejudices) nor in the institutional setting (as when an authoritarian leader has such enormous power over the individuals who serve on his policy-planning committees that they are intimidated into becoming sycophants). Along with these well known sources of defective judgment, we must consider what happens whenever a small body of decision makers becomes a cohesive group. We know that group psychology has its own dynamics and that interactions within a friendly group often are not conducive to critical thinking. At times, the striving for group concurrence can become so dominant that it interferes with adequate problem-solving, prevents the elaboration of alternative courses of action, and inhibits independent judgment, even when the decision makers are conscientious statesmen trying to make the best possible decisions for their country or for all of humanity.

In my case studies of cohesive policy-making committees I have repeatedly noted eight main symptoms of groupthink, several of which I have already illustrated in the foregoing discussion: (1) a shared illusion of invulnerability, which leads to an extraordinary degree of overoptimism and risk-taking; (2) manifestations of direct pressure on individuals who express disagreement with or doubt about the majority view, making it clear that dissent is contrary to the expected behavior of loyal group members; (3) fear of disapproval for deviating from the group consensus, which leads each member to avoid voicing his misgivings and even to minimize to himself the importance of his doubts when most of the others seem to agree on a proposed course of action; (4) a shared illusion of unanimity within the group concerning all the main judgments expressed by members who speak in favor of the majority view (partly resulting from the preceding symptom, which contributes to the false assumption that any individual who remains silent during any part of the discussion is in full accord with what the others are saying); (5) stereotyped views of the enemy leaders as evil, often accompanied by the assumption that they are too weak or too stupid to deal effectively with whatever risky attempts are made to outdo them; (6) an unquestioned belief in the inherent morality of the in-group, which inclines the members to ignore the ethical or moral consequences of their decisions; (7) the emergence of self-appointed mind guards within the group—members who take it upon themselves to protect the leader and fellow members from adverse information that may prevent them from being able to continue their shared sense of complacency about the effectiveness and morality of past decisions; and (8) shared efforts to construct rationalizations in order to be able to ignore warnings and other forms of negative feedback, which, if taken seriously, would lead the members to reconsider the assumptions they continue to take for granted each time they recommit themselves to their past policy decisions.

When most or all of these interrelated symptoms are displayed by a group of executives, a detailed study of their deliberations is likely to reveal additional symptoms that are, in effect, poor decision-making practices because they lead to inadequate solutions to the problems under discussion. Among the main symptoms of inadequate problem-solving are the following:

First, the discussions are limited to a few alternative courses of action (often only two alternatives) without an initial survey of all the various alternatives that may be worthy of consideration.

Second, the group fails to reexamine the course of action initially preferred by the majority of members from the standpoint of nonobvious risks and drawbacks that had not been considered when it was originally selected.

Third, the group fails to reexamine any of the courses of action initially rejected by the majority of members from the standpoint of nonobvious gains that may have been overlooked and ways of reducing the seemingly prohibitive costs or risks that had made these alternatives appear to be inferior.

Fourth, little or no attempt is made to obtain information from experts within the same organization who may be able to supply more precise estimates of potential losses and gains to be expected from alternative courses of actions, particularly on matters about which none of the members of the group are well informed.

Fifth, selective bias is shown in the way the group reacts to factual information and relevant judgments from the mass media or from outside experts. The members show positive interest in facts and opinions that support their initially preferred policy and take up time in their meetings to discuss them, whereas they tend to ignore facts and opinions that do not support their initially preferred policy.

Sixth, the members of the group spend little time thinking about how the chosen policy or set of plans may be unintentionally hindered by bureaucratic inertia, be deliberately sabotaged by opponents, or be temporarily derailed by common accidents that happen to well laid plans; consequently, they fail to work out contingency plans to cope with setbacks that could endanger the overall success of the decision.

All six of these defects are products of groupthink. These same inadequacies can arise from other causes such as erroneous intelligence, informational overloads, fatigue, blinding prejudice, ignorance, panic. Whether produced by groupthink or by other causes, a decision that suffers from these defects has little chance of long-run success. When the group members try to implement their poorly worked out plans, they are soon shocked to find themselves caught in one new crisis after another, as they are forced to work out from scratch the solutions to vital questions about all the obstacles to be overcome—questions that should have been anticipated beforehand. Their poorly constructed decision, like a defective old auto that is starting to fall apart, is barely kept running by hastily patching it up with whatever ill-fitting spare parts happen to be at hand. For a time, the owners may loyally insist that they are still operating a solidly dependable vehicle, ignoring as long as possible each new sign that another part is starting to fail. But only extraordinary good luck can save them from the ultimate humiliation of seeing the whole thing fall so completely to pieces that it has to be abandoned as a total loss.

I am not implying that all cohesive groups necessarily suffer from groupthink. All in-groups may have a mild tendency toward groupthink, displaying one or another of the symptoms from time to time, but it need not be so dominant as to influence the quality of the final decision of the members. The term *groupthink* also does not imply that there is anything necessarily inefficient or harmful about group decisions in general. On the contrary, a group whose members have properly defined roles, with methodical procedures to follow in pursuing a critical inquiry, is probably capable of making better decisions than is any individual in the group who works on the problem alone. However, the great gains to be obtained from decision-making groups are often lost because of powerful psychological pressures that arise when the members work together, share the same set of values, and, above all, face a crisis situation where everyone is subjected to a high degree of stress. In these circumstances, as conformity pressures begin to dominate, groupthink and its attendant deterioration in the quality of decision-making set in.

Time and again in the case studies of major historic fiascos, I have encountered evidence that like-minded men working in concert have a great many assets for making adequate decisions but also are subjected to group processes that have serious liabilities. Under certain conditions, which I believe we can start to specify, the liabilities can outweigh the assets. A central theme of my analysis then can be summarized briefly in a somewhat oversimplified generalization, which I offer in the spirit of Parkinson's laws. The main hypothesis concerning groupthink is this: The more amiability and esprit de corps among the members of an in-group of policy makers the greater the danger that independent critical thinking will be replaced by groupthink, which is likely to result in irrational and dehumanizing actions directed at out-groups.

Since this groupthink hypothesis has not yet been tested systematically, we must regard it as merely a suggestive generalization inferred from a small number of historical case studies. Still, one should not be inhibited, it seems to me, from drawing tentative inferences—as long as we label them as such—concerning the conditions that promote groupthink and the potentially effective means for preventing those conditions from arising.

Can we specify the conditions that help to prevent groupthink? Certainly not with any degree of certainty at present. But strong indications from comparative studies of good versus poor governmental decisions suggest a number of relevant hypotheses. So far, I have had the opportunity to examine only a small number of policy decisions, contrasting several major fiascos with two major decisions that provide counterpoint examples. One of the latter was the course of action decided upon by the Kennedy administration in October 1962, during the Cuban missile crisis. This decision involved the same cast of characters as the Bay of Pigs fiasco in 1961. My study of the Cuban missile crisis suggests that groupthink tendencies can be prevented by certain leadership practices that promote independent thinking. Another such counterpoint example I have looked into is the work of the small planning committees in the Truman administration that evolved the Marshall Plan in 1948. Like the White House group that developed the plan for coping with the Cuban missile crisis, these groups made realistic appraisals of how the Soviet Union and other out-groups were likely to respond to the various alternatives being considered, instead of relying on crude stereotypes and slogans.

One fundamental condition that appears to have an adverse effect on the quality of many vital decisions is secrecy. Frequently, only members of a small group of high-level officials are allowed to be in on a decision concerning the use of military force. The decision-making group is insulated from the judgments of experts and other qualified associates who, as outsiders, are not permitted to know anything about the new policies under discussion until after a final decision has been made. In the United States government there is a rule that even among men who have the highest security clearance, no one should be consulted or informed when a secret policy is up for discussion unless it is absolutely essential for him to know about it.

Small groups are highly susceptible to concurrence-seeking tendencies that interfere with critical thinking during crisis periods, especially if they restrict their discussions to the group itself. The chances of encountering effective, independent evaluations are greatest when the decision is openly discussed among varying groups who have different types of expertise, all of whom examine the decision and its probable outcomes from the standpoint of somewhat different value orientations. But when a decision is closed—confined to a small group—the chances of encountering anyone who can break up a premature emerging consensus is reduced. Similarly, insulation of the decision-making group greatly reduces the chances that unwarranted stereotypes and slogans shared by members of the group will be challenged before it is too late to avert a fiasco.

I am speaking of more than isolation from out-groups. It is a matter of isolation from other potential in-group members, such as respected associates in high positions within the government who are not members of the specific policy-making group. If brought into the meetings, these nonmembers may be capable of presenting a fresh point of view and of raising critical questions that may be overlooked by the in-group. Their comments may induce members of the group to reconsider their assumptions.

If group isolation promotes groupthink, with its consequent mindless and dehumanized policies, then we should see what may be done to help prevent insulation of the members of a policy planning group. First, each member of the planning group can be expected to discuss the deliberations with associates in his home office—assuming that he has associates who can be trusted—and then to report back to the planning group the reactions obtained from this source of relatively independent thinkers.

A second safeguard is to invite to each meeting one or more outside experts or qualified colleagues who are not core members of the policy-making group, including representatives from other branches of the government who are known to be critical thinkers, sensitive to moral issues, and capable of presenting their ideas effectively. Such outsiders were, in fact, deliberately brought into the Executive Committee meetings during the Cuban missile crisis and were encouraged to express their objections openly so that the group could debate them. This atmosphere was quite different from the one that prevailed throughout the Bay of Pigs planning sessions, which were restricted to the same small group of advisers and were dominated by the two CIA leaders who had developed the ill-fated plan. On one occasion, Chester Bowles was present as under-secretary of state to replace his chief, Rusk, who had to attend a meeting abroad. But Bowles was never asked about his reactions. He sat there silently, listening with horror to a discussion based on what he regarded as incredibly foolish and dangerous assumptions. After he left the meeting, he wrote down his objections in a memorandum to Rusk, who promptly buried it in the State Department files. In this instance, Rusk took on the role of what I call a self-appointed mind guard.

Third, a multiple-group procedure can be instituted so that instead of having only a single group work on a given major policy problem from beginning to end, responsibility is assigned to several planning and evaluation groups, each carrying out its deliberations, concurrently or successively, under a different leader. At times, the separate groups can be brought together to hammer out their differences, a procedure which would also help to reduce the chances that the decision makers will evolve a consensus based on shared miscalculations and illusory assumptions.

Now we turn to factors other than isolation that determine whether groupthink tendencies will predominate in a cohesive policy-making group. In the light of my comparative case studies, the following additional prescriptions can be added to the three already mentioned as possible antidotes for counteracting groupthink.

Fourth, new leadership procedures and traditions may be established so that the leader abstains from presenting his own position at the outset to avoid setting a norm that evokes conformity before the issues are fully explored by the members. For example, the leader may deliberately absent himself from the initial policy-making discussions, as Kennedy did when the White House Executive Committee began to meet during the Cuban missile crisis. In order to introduce this corrective procedure, of course, the leader has to be willing to renounce some of his traditional prerogatives.

Fifth, at every general meeting of the group, whenever the agenda calls for evaluation of policy alternatives, at least one member can be assigned the role of devil's advocate, to function like a good lawyer in challenging the testimony of all those who advocate the majority position. During the Cuban missile crisis, Kennedy gave his brother, the attorney general, the mission of playing devil's advocate, with seemingly excellent results in breaking up a premature consensus. When this devil's advocate's role is performed well, it requires the members of the group to examine carefully the pros and cons of policy alternatives before they agree upon the best course of action.

Sixth, throughout all the group meetings, each member can be assigned the primary role of critical evaluator of policy alternatives, a role which takes precedence over any factional loyalties and over the traditional forms of deference or politeness that often incline a man to remain silent when he objects to someone else's cherished ideas. This proposed practice, which could not be instituted unless it were wholeheartedly approved, initiated, and reinforced by the President and other top executives in the hierarchy, can help to counteract the spontaneous group pressures for concurrence-seeking. It should certainly prevent an illusion of unanimity from bolstering a premature consensus.

Seventh, whenever the policy issue involves relations with a rival nation or organization, at least part of a session can be devoted to surveying recent warning signals from the rivals, using special audiovisual techniques or psychodramatic role-playing, to stimulate the policy makers to construct alternative scenarios regarding the rival's intentions. In order to counteract the members' shared illusions of invulnerability and tendency to ignore or explain away any warning signals that interfere with a complacent outlook, this special effort may be required to induce them to become sharply aware of the potential risks and the need for making realistic contingency plans.

Eighth, after a preliminary consensus is reached concerning what seems to be the best policy alternative, a special session can be held at which every member is expected to express as vividly as he can all his residual doubts and to rethink the entire issue before making a definitive choice. This second-chance meeting should be held before the group commits itself by taking a final vote.

Two main conclusions are suggested by the case studies of foreign policy decisions: along with other sources of error in decision-making, the symptoms of groupthink are likely to occur from time to time within cohesive small groups of policy makers; and the most corrosive symptoms of groupthink are preventable by eliminating group insulation, overdirective leadership practices, and other conditions that foster premature concurrence-seeking.

Sometimes it may even be useful for one of the policy makers to ask at the right moment, before a decision is definitely made, "Are we allowing ourselves to become victims of groupthink?" I am not proposing that this question should be placed on the agenda or that the members should try to conduct a group therapy session, comparable to parlor psychoanalysis. Rather, I have in mind enabling some policy makers to adopt a psychological set that inclines them to raise critical questions whenever there are signs of undue complacency or premature consensus. One such question has to do with the consensus itself. A leader who is aware of the symptoms of groupthink, for example, may say, "Before we assume that everyone agrees with this proposed strategy, let's hear from those who haven't said anything yet, so that we can get all points of view onto the table."

With these considerations in mind, I suggest that awareness of shared illusions, rationalizations, and other symptoms fostered by small-group interaction may curtail the influence of groupthink in policy-making groups, including those that meet in the White House. Here we may apply George Santayana's well known adage: "Those who cannot remember the past are condemned to repeat it." Perhaps with a better understanding of group dynamics we can avoid repeating the history of the Vietnam war, with its indiscriminate destruction of native villages and its My Lai massacres.

* * *

Additional case studies of groupthink, an expanded discussion of its implications, and some specific recommendations for its prevention are presented in Irving L. Janis, *Victims of Groupthink* (Boston: Houghton Mifflin, 1972).

Behavioral Study of Obedience

Stanley Milgram

Obedience is as basic an element in the structure of social life as one can point to. Some system of authority is a requirement of all communal living, and it is only the man dwelling in isolation who is not forced to respond, through defiance or submission, to the commands of others. Obedience, as a determinant of behavior, is of particular relevance to our time. It has been reliably established that from 1933–45 millions of innocent persons were systematically slaughtered on command. Gas chambers were built, death camps were guarded, daily quotas of corpses were produced with the same efficiency as the manufacture of appliances. These inhumane policies may have originated in the mind of a single person, but they could only be carried out on a massive scale if a very large number of persons obeyed orders.

Obedience is the psychological mechanism that links individual action to political purpose. It is the dispositional cement that binds men to systems of authority. Facts of recent history and observation in daily life suggest that for many persons obedience may be a deeply ingrained behavior tendency, indeed, a prepotent impulse overriding training in ethics, sympathy, and moral conduct. C. P. Snow points to its importance when he writes:

When you think of the long and gloomy history of man, you will find more hideous crimes have been committed in the name of obedience than have ever been committed in the name of rebellion. If you doubt that, read William Shirer's "Rise and Fall of the Third Reich." The German Officer Corps were brought up in the most rigorous code of obedience . . . in the name of obedi-

Abridged from *Journal of Abnormal and Social Psychology*, 1963, *67*, 371–378.

ence they were party to, and assisted in, the most wicked large scale actions in the history of the world.[1]

While the particular form of obedience dealt with in the present study has its antecedents in these episodes, it must not be thought all obedience entails acts of aggression against others. Obedience serves numerous productive functions. Indeed, the very life of society is predicated on its existence. Obedience may be ennobling and educative and refer to acts of charity and kindness, as well as to destruction.

GENERAL PROCEDURE

A procedure was devised which seems useful as a tool for studying obedience.[2] It consists of ordering a naive subject to administer electric shock to a victim. A stimulated shock generator is used, with 30 clearly marked voltage levels that range from 15 to 450 volts. The instrument bears verbal designations that range from Slight Shock to Danger: Severe Shock. The responses of the victim, who is a trained confederate of the experimenter, are standardized. The orders to administer shocks are given to the naive subject in the context of a "learning experiment" ostensibly set up to study the effects of punishment on memory. As the experiment proceeds the naive subject is commanded to administer increasingly more intense shocks to the victim, even to the point of reaching the level marked Danger: Severe Shock. Internal resistances become stronger, and at a certain point the subject refuses to go on with the experiment. Behavior prior to this rupture is considered "obedience," in that the subject complies with the commands of the experimenter. The point of rupture is the act of disobedience. A quantitative value is assigned to the subject's performance based on the maximum intensity shock he is willing to administer before he refuses to participate further. Thus for any particular subject and for any particular experimental condition the degree of obedience may be specified with a numerical value. The crux of the study is to systematically vary the factors believed to alter the degree of obedience to the experimental commands.

The technique allows important variables to be manipulated at several points in the experiment. One may vary aspects of the source of command, content and form of command, instrumentalities for its execution, target object, general social setting, etc. The problem, therefore, is not one of designing increasingly more numerous experimental conditions, but of selecting those that best illuminate the *process* of obedience from the sociopsychological standpoint.

[1] C. P. Snow, "Either-or," *Progressive* (Feb. 1961), p. 24.

[2] S. Milgram, "Dynamics of obedience" (Washington: National Science Foundation, 25 January 1961.) (Mimeo.)

METHOD

SUBJECTS

The subjects were 40 males between the ages of 20 and 50, drawn from New Haven and the surrounding communities. Subjects were obtained by a newspaper advertisement and direct mail solicitation. Those who responded to the appeal believed they were to participate in a study of memory and learning at Yale University. A wide range of occupations is represented in the sample. Typical subjects were postal clerks, high school teachers, salesmen, engineers, and laborers. Subjects ranged in educational level from one who had not finished elementary school, to those who had doctorate and other professional degrees. They were paid $4.50 for their participation in the experiment. However, subjects were told that payment was simply for coming to the laboratory, and that the money was theirs no matter what happened after they arrived.

PERSONNEL AND LOCALE

The experiment was conducted on the grounds of Yale University in the elegant interaction laboratory. (This detail is relevant to the perceived legitimacy of the experiment. In further variations, the experiment was dissociated from the university, with consequences for performance.) The role of experimenter was played by a 31-year-old high school teacher of biology. His manner was impassive, and his appearance somewhat stern throughout the experiment. He was dressed in a gray technician's coat. The victim was played by a 47-year-old accountant, trained for the role; he was of Irish-American stock, whom most observers found mild-mannered and likable.

PROCEDURE

One naive subject and one victim (an accomplice) performed in each experiment. A pretext had to be devised that would justify the administration of electric shock by the naive subject. This was effectively accomplished by the cover story. After a general introduction on the presumed relation between punishment and learning, subjects were told:

> But actually, we know *very little* about the effect of punishment on learning, because almost no truly scientific studies have been made of it in human beings.
>
> For instance, we don't know how *much* punishment is best for learning—and we don't know how much difference it makes as to who is giving the punishment, whether an adult learns best from a younger or an older person than himself—or many things of that sort.
>
> So in this study we are bringing together a number of adults of different occupations and ages. And we're asking some of them to be teachers and some of them to be learners.

We want to find out just what effect different people have on each other as teachers and learners, and also what effect *punishment* will have on learning in this situation.

Therefore, I'm going to ask one of you to be the teacher here tonight and the other one to be the learner.

Does either of you have a preference?

Subjects then drew slips of paper from a hat to determine who would be the teacher and who would be the learner in the experiment. The drawing was rigged so that the naive subject was always the teacher and the accomplice always the learner. (Both slips contained the word "Teacher.") Immediately after the drawing, the teacher and learner were taken to an adjacent room and the learner was strapped into an "electric chair" apparatus.

The experimenter explained that the straps were to prevent excessive movement while the learner was being shocked. The effect was to make it impossible for him to escape from the situation. An electrode was attached to the learner's wrist, and electrode paste was applied "to avoid blisters and burns." Subjects were told that the electrode was attached to the shock generator in the adjoining room.

In order to improve credibility the experimenter declared, in response to a question by the learner: "Although the shocks can be extremely painful, they cause no permanent tissue damage."

Learning task. The lesson administered by the subject was a paired-associate learning task. The subject read a series of word pairs to the learner, and then read the first word of the pair along with four terms. The learner was to indicate which of the four terms had originally been paired with the first word. He communicated his answer by pressing one of four switches in front of him, which in turn lit up one of four numbered quadrants in an answer-box located atop the shock generator.

Shock generator. The instrument panel consists of 30 lever switches set in a horizontal line. Each switch is clearly labeled with a voltage designation that ranges from 15 to 450 volts. There is a 15-volt increment from one switch to the next going from left to right. In addition, the following verbal designations are clearly indicated for groups of four switches going from left to right: Slight Shock, Moderate Shock, Strong Shock, Very Strong Shock, Intense Shock, Extreme Intensity Shock, Danger: Severe Shock. (Two switches after this last designation are simply marked XXX.)

Upon depressing a switch: a pilot light corresponding to each switch is illuminated in bright red; an electric buzzing is heard; an electric blue light, labeled "voltage energizer," flashes; the dial on the voltage meter swings to the right; various relay clicks are sounded.

The upper left-hand corner of the generator is labeled Shock Generator, Type ZLB, Dyson Instrument Company, Waltham, Mass. Output 15 Volts-450 Volts.

Details of the instrument were carefully handled to insure an appearance of authenticity. The panel was engraved by precision industrial engravers, and all components were of high quality. No subject in the experiment suspected that the instrument was merely a simulated shock generator.

Sample shock. Each naive subject is given a sample shock on the shock generator, prior to beginning his run as teacher. This shock is always 45 volts, and is applied by pressing the third switch of the generator. The shock is applied to the wrist of the naive subject, and has its source in a 45-volt battery wired into the generator. This further convinces the subject of the authenticity of the generator.

Shock instructions. The subject is told to administer a shock to the learner each time he gives a wrong response. Moreover—and this is the key command—the subject is instructed to "move one level higher on the shock generator each time the learner flashes a wrong answer." He is also instructed to announce the voltage level before administering a shock. This serves to continually remind subjects of the increasing intensity of shocks administered to the learner.

Preliminary and regular run. Pretests revealed that the procedure of reading words and administering shocks requires some practice before it can be handled smoothly. Therefore, immediately preceding the regular run, the teacher is given a preliminary series of 10 words to read to the learner. There are 3 neutral words in the practice series (i.e., words that the learner answers correctly), so that shocks are administered for 7 of the words, with the maximum shock at 105 volts (moderate shock). Almost all subjects master the procedure by the time the preliminary run is over.

Subjects are then presented with a second list, and are told that the procedure is the same as for the first list; the experimenter adds, however:

> When you get to the bottom of the list, repeat it over again, and continue giving shocks, until the learner has learned all the pairs correctly.

The experimenter instructs the subject to,

> start from 15 volts and increase the shock level one step each time the learner gives a wrong answer.

Feedback from the victim. In all conditions the learner gives a predetermined set of responses to the word pair test, based on a schedule of approximately three wrong answers to one correct answer. In the present experimental condition no vocal response or other sign of protest is heard from the learner until Shock Level 300 is reached. When the 300-volt shock is administered, the learner pounds on the wall of the room in which he is bound to the electric chair. The pounding can be heard by the subject. From this point on, the learner's answers no longer appear on the four-way panel.

At this juncture, subjects ordinarily turn to the experimenter for guidance. The experimenter instructs the subject to treat the absence of a response as a wrong answer, and to shock the subject according to the usual schedule. He advises the subjects to allow 5–10 seconds before considering no response as a wrong answer, and to increase the shock level one step each time the learner fails to respond correctly. The learner's pounding is repeated after the 315-volt shock is administered; afterwards he is not heard from, nor do his answers reappear on the four-way signal box.

Experimenter feedback. At various points in the experiment the subject may turn to the experimenter for advice on whether he should continue to administer shocks. Or he may indicate that he does not wish to go on. It was important to standardize the experimenter's responses to these inquiries and reactions.

If the subject indicated his unwillingness to go on, the experimenter responded with a sequence of "prods," using as many as necessary to bring the subject into line.

Prod 1: Please continue, *or* Please go on.
Prod 2: The experiment requires that you continue.
Prod 3: It is absolutely essential that you continue.
Prod 4: You have no other choice, you *must* go on.

The prods were always made in sequence: Only if Prod 1 had been unsuccessful, could Prod 2 be used. If the subject refused to obey the experimenter after Prod 4, the experiment was terminated. The experimenter's tone of voice was at all times firm, but not impolite. The sequence was begun anew on each occasion that the subject balked or showed reluctance to follow orders.

Special prods. If the subject asked if the learner was liable to suffer permanent physical injury, the experimenter said:

Although the shocks may be painful, there is no permanent tissue damage, so please go on. [Followed by Prods 2, 3, and 4 if necessary.]

If the subject said that the learner did not want to go on, the experimenter replied:

Whether the learner likes it or not, you must go on until he has learned all the word pairs correctly. So please go on. [Followed by Prods 2, 3, and 4 if necessary.]

MEASURES

The primary measure for any subject is the maximum shock he administers before he refuses to go any further. In principle this may vary from 0 (for a subject who refuses to administer even the first shock) to 30 (for a subject who administers the highest shock on the generator). A subject who breaks off the experiment at any point prior to administering the thirtieth shock level is termed a *defiant* subject. One who complies with experimental commands fully, and proceeds to administer all shock levels commanded, is termed an *obedient* subject.

Further records. With few exceptions, experimental sessions were recorded on magnetic tape. Occasional photographs were taken through one-way mirrors. Notes were kept on any unusual behavior occurring during the course of the experiments. On occasion, additional observers were directed to write objective descriptions of the subjects' behavior. The latency and duration of shocks were measured by accurate timing devices.

Interview and dehoax. Following the experiment, subjects were interviewed; open-ended questions, projective measures, and attitude scales were employed. After the interview, procedures were undertaken to assure that the subject would leave the laboratory in a state of well being. A friendly reconciliation was arranged between the subject and the victim, and an effort was made to reduce any tensions that arose as a result of the experiment.

RESULTS

PRELIMINARY NOTIONS

Before giving an account of the experimental results, it is instructive to consider how persons predict others will perform when commanded to administer powerful shocks to another person. Fourteen Yale seniors, all psychology majors, were provided with a detailed description of the experimental situation. They were asked to reflect carefully on it, and to predict the behavior of 100 hypothetical subjects. More specifically, they were instructed to plot the distribution of obedience of "100 Americans of diverse occupations, and ranging in age from 20 to 50 years," who were placed in the experimental situation.

There was considerable agreement among the respondents on the expected behavior of hypothetical subjects. All respondents predicted that only an insignificant minority would go through to the end of the shock series. (The estimates ranged from 0 to 3%; i.e., the most "pessimistic" member of the class predicted that of 100 persons, 3 would continue through to the most potent shock available on the shock generator—450 volts.) The class mean was 1.2%. The question was also posed informally to colleagues of the author, and the most general feeling was that few if any subjects would go beyond the designation Very Strong Shock.

RESULT OF EXPERIMENT I

With few exceptions subjects were convinced of the reality of the experimental situation, that they were administering shocks to another person, and the most potent shocks were extremely painful. In the post-experimental interview subjects were asked: "How painful to the learner were the last few shocks that you administered to him?" Subjects were instructed to indicate their answers on a printed 14-point scale ranging from "Not at all painful" to "Extremely painful." The modal response was 14 (Extremely painful) with the mean at 13.42.

Many subjects showed signs of nervousness in the experimental situation, and especially upon administering the more powerful shocks. In a large number of cases the degree of tension reached extremes that are rarely seen in sociopsychological laboratory studies. Subjects were observed to sweat, tremble, stutter, bite their lips, groan, and dig their fingernails into their flesh. These were characteristic rather than exceptional responses to the experiment.

One sign of tension was the regular occurrence of nervous laughing fits. Fourteen of the 40 subjects showed definite signs of nervous laughter and smiling. The laughter seemed entirely out of place, even bizarre. Full-blown, uncontrollable seizures were observed for 3 subjects. On one occasion we observed a seizure so violently convulsive that it was necessary to call a halt to the experiment. The subject, a 46-year-old encyclopedia salesman, was seriously embarrassed by his untoward and uncontrollable behavior. In the post-experimental interviews subjects took pains to point out that they were not sadistic types, and that the laughter did not mean they enjoyed shocking the victim.

It had been conjectured that persons would not, in general, agree to administer shocks beyond the level designated as Very Strong Shock. The distribution of maximum shocks for this experiment is shown in Table 1. The obtained distribution of scores deviates radically from the prediction.

Upon command of the experimenter, each of the 40 subjects went beyond the expected breakoff point. No subject stopped prior to administering Shock Level 20. (At this level—300 volts—the victim kicks on the wall and no longer provides answers to the teacher's multiple-choice questions.)

Of the 40 subjects, 5 refused to obey the experimental commands beyond the 300-volt level. Four more subjects administered one further shock, and then refused to go on. Two broke off at the 330-volt level, and 1 each at 345, 360, and 375 volts. Thus a total of 14 subjects defied the experimenter. It is instructive to reprint their remarks at the point of defiance, as transcribed from the tape recordings:

[0124] I think he's trying to communicate, he's knocking. . . . Well it's not fair to shock the guy . . . these are terrific volts. I don't think this is very humane. . . . Oh, I can't go on with this; no, this isn't right. It's a hell of an experiment. The guy is suffering in there. No, I don't want to go on. This is crazy. [Subject refused to administer more shocks.]

[0123] He's banging in there. I'm gonna chicken out. I'd like to continue, but I can't do that to a man. . . . I'm sorry I can't do that to a man. I'll hurt his heart. You take your check. . . . No really, I couldn't do it.

These subjects were frequently in a highly agitated and even angered state. Sometimes, verbal protest was at a minimum, and the subject simply got up from his chair in front of the shock generator, and indicated that he wished to leave the laboratory.

TABLE 1
DISTRIBUTION OF BREAKOFF POINTS

Verbal designation and voltage indication	*Number of subjects for whom this was maximum shock*
Slight Shock	
15	0
30	0
45	0
60	0
Moderate Shock	
75	0
90	0
105	0
120	0
Strong Shock	
135	0
150	0
165	0
180	0
Very Strong Shock	
195	0
210	0
225	0
240	0
Intense Shock	
255	0
270	0
285	0
300	5
Extreme Intensity Shock	
315	4
330	2
345	1
360	1
Danger: Severe Shock	
375	1
390	0
405	0
420	0
XXX	
435	0
450	26

Of the 40 subjects, 26 obeyed the orders of the experimenter to the end, proceeding to punish the victim until they reached the most potent shock available on the shock generator. At that point, the experimenter called a halt to the session. (The maximum shock is labeled 450 volts, and is two steps beyond the designation: Danger: Severe Shock.) Although obedient subjects continued to administer shocks, they often did so under extreme stress. Some expressed reluctance to administer shocks beyond the 300-volt level, and displayed fears similar to those who defied the experimenter; yet they obeyed.

After the maximum shocks had been delivered, and the experimenter called a halt to the proceedings, many obedient subjects heaved sighs of relief, mopped their brows, rubbed their fingers over their eyes, or nervously fumbled cigarettes. Some shook their heads, apparently in regret. Some subjects had remained calm throughout the experiment; and displayed only minimal signs of tension from beginning to end.

DISCUSSION

The experiment yielded two findings that were surprising. The first finding concerns the sheer strength of obedient tendencies manifested in this situation. Subjects have learned from childhood that it is a fundamental breach of moral conduct to hurt another person against his will. Yet, 26 subjects abandon this tenet in following the instructions of an authority who has no special powers to enforce his commands. To disobey would bring no material loss to the subject; no punishment would ensue. It is clear from the remarks and outward behavior of many participants that in punishing the victim they are often acting against their own values. Subjects often expressed deep disapproval of shocking a man in the face of his objections, and others denounced it as stupid and senseless. Yet the majority complied with the experimental commands. This outcome was surprising from two perspectives: first, from the standpoint of predictions made in the questionnaire described earlier. (Here, however, it is possible that the remoteness of the respondents from the actual situation, and the difficulty of conveying to them the concrete details of the experiment, could account for the serious underestimation of obedience.)

But the results were also unexpected to persons who observed the experiment in progress, through one-way mirrors. Observers often uttered expressions of disbelief upon seeing a subject administer more powerful shocks to the victim. These persons had a full acquaintance with the details of the situation, and yet systematically underestimated the amount of obedience that subjects would display.

The second unanticipated effect was the extraordinary tension generated by the procedures. One might suppose that a subject would simply break off or continue as his conscience dictated. Yet, this is very far from what happened. There were striking reactions of tension and emotional strain. One observer related:

> I observed a mature and initially poised businessman enter the laboratory smiling and confident. Within 20 minutes he was reduced to a twitching, stuttering wreck, who was rapidly approaching a point of nervous collapse. He constantly pulled on his earlobe, and twisted his hands. At one point he pushed his fist into his forehead and muttered: "Oh God, let's stop it." And yet he continued to respond to every word of the experimenter, and obeyed to the end.

Any understanding of the phenomenon of obedience must rest on an analysis of the particular conditions in which it occurs. The following features of the experiment go some distance in explaining the high amount of obedience observed in the situation.

1. The experiment is sponsored by and takes place on the grounds of an institution of unimpeachable reputation, Yale University. It may be reasonably presumed that the personnel are competent and reputable. The importance of this background authority has since been studied by conducting a series of experiments outside of New Haven, and without any visible ties to the university.

2. The experiment is, on the face of it, designed to attain a worthy purpose—advancement of knowledge about learning and memory. Obedience occurs not as an end in itself, but as an instrumental element in a situation that the subject construes as significant, and meaningful. He may not be able to see its full significance, but he may properly assume that the experimenter does.

3. The subject perceives that the victim has voluntarily submitted to the authority system of the experimenter. He is not (at first) an unwilling captive impressed for involuntary service. He has taken the trouble to come to the laboratory presumably to aid the experimental research. That he later becomes an involuntary subject does not alter the fact that, initially, he consented to participate without qualification. Thus he has in some degree incurred an obligation toward the experimenter.

4. The subject, too, has entered the experiment voluntarily, and perceives himself under obligation to aid the experimenter. He has made a commitment, and to disrupt the experiment is a repudiation of this initial promise of aid.

5. Certain features of the procedure strengthen the subject's sense of obligation to the experimenter. For one, he has been paid for coming to the laboratory. In part this is canceled out by the experimenter's statement that:

Of course, as in all experiments, the money is yours simply for coming to the laboratory. From this point on, no matter what happens, the money is yours.[3]

6. From the subject's standpoint, the fact that he is the teacher and the other man the learner is purely a chance consequence (it is determined by drawing lots) and he, the subject, ran the same risk as the other man in being assigned the role of learner. Since the assignment of positions in the experiment was achieved by fair means, the learner is deprived of any basis of complaint on this count. (A similar situation obtains in Army units, in which—in the absence of volunteers—a particularly dangerous mission may be assigned by drawing lots, and the unlucky soldier is expected to bear his misfortune with sportsmanship.)

7. There is, at best, ambiguity with regard to the prerogatives of a psychologist and the corresponding rights of his subject. There is a vagueness of expectation concerning what a psychologist may require of his subject, and when he is overstepping acceptable limits. Moreover, the experiment occurs in a closed setting, and thus provides no opportunity for the subject to remove these ambiguities by discussion with others. There are few standards that seem directly applicable to the situation, which is a novel one for most subjects.

8. The subjects are assured that the shocks administered to the subject are "painful but not dangerous." Thus they assume that the discomfort caused the victim is momentary, while the scientific gains resulting from the experiment are enduring.

9. Through Shock Level 20 the victim continues to provide answers on the signal box. The subject may construe this as a sign that the victim is still willing to "play the game." It is only after Shock Level 20 that the victim repudiates the rules completely, refusing to answer further.

These features help to explain the high amount of obedience obtained in this experiment. Many of the arguments raised need not remain matters of speculation, but can be reduced to testable propositions to be confirmed or disproved by further experiments.

The following features of the experiment concern the nature of the conflict which the subject faces.

10. The subject is placed in a position in which he must respond to the competing demands of two persons: the experimenter and the victim. The conflict must be resolved by meeting the demands of one or the other; satisfaction of the victim and the experimenter are mutually exclusive. Moreover, the resolution must take the form of a highly visible action, that of continuing to shock the victim or breaking off the experi-

[3] Forty-three subjects, undergraduates at Yale University, were run in the experiment without payment. The results are very similar to those obtained with paid subjects.

ment. Thus the subject is forced into a public conflict that does not permit any completely satisfactory solution.

11. While the demands of the experimenter carry the weight of scientific authority, the demands of the victim spring from his personal experience of pain and suffering. The two claims need not be regarded as equally pressing and legitimate. The experimenter seeks an abstract scientific datum; the victim cries out for relief from physical suffering caused by the subject's actions.

12. The experiment gives the subject little time for reflection. The conflict comes on rapidly. It is only minutes after the subject has been seated before the shock generator that the victim begins his protests. Moreover, the subject perceives that he has gone through but two-thirds of the shock levels at the time the subject's first protests are heard. Thus he understands that the conflict will have a persistent aspect to it, and may well become more intense as increasingly more powerful shocks are required. The rapidity with which the conflict descends on the subject, and his realization that it is predictably recurrent may well be sources of tension to him.

13. At a more general level, the conflict stems from the opposition of two deeply ingrained behavior dispositions: first, the disposition not to harm other people, and second, the tendency to obey those whom we perceive to be legitimate authorities.

* * *

For a full account of this research, see Stanley Milgram, *Obedience to Authority: An Experimental View* (New York: Harper & Row, 1974).

HELPING

Psychologists and other social scientists have traditionally devoted much more of their attention to hurting than to helping. A content analysis of the psychological literature found that more than four times as many studies during the period 1930–1960 were devoted to "negative" aspects (e.g., aggression, hostility, and prejudice) than to "positive" aspects (e.g., altruism, cooperation, and trust) of social behavior.[1] This lopsidedness seems to have resulted in part from a pragmatic philosophy—if aggression, hostility, and prejudice are our most pressing social problems, then they are what we must study. An additional reason for the discrepancy was a theoretical one. Aggression and hostility could easily be understood within the reigning frameworks of reinforcement theory and psychoanalysis, each of which preached its own brand of basic human selfishness. Altruistic and sympathetic behaviors, in which people exert time and effort and take personal risks for the sake of others, were less easily explained within these frameworks. Within the past decade, however, there has been a great surge of research interest in altruism and helping behavior. Theoretical frameworks are being expanded in order to accommodate these previously baffling phenomena.

Helping is sometimes encouraged by social pressures. Children are taught to help those who are in need, and the Good Samaritan is held up as a model of good behavior. Telethons and other charity drives try to harness conformity pressures in the service of their causes. But conformity may also lead to failures to help. The ingenious series of experiments conducted by Bibb Latané and John Darley converge on the conclusion that the more witnesses there are to an emergency, the less likely any one of them will be to help. In such situations social pressures seem to lull people to apathy, instead of spurring them to action. Thus people's

[1] Lauren G. Wispé, "A quantitative analysis of studies of positive and negative social behavior." Unpublished manuscript, University of Oklahoma, 1974.

failures to come to the aid of victims are frequently due not to personality defects or lack of moral fiber, but rather to the structure of the emergency situations themselves.

The research reported by Carl Fellner and John Marshall concerns an act of helping of great magnitude—the donation of a vital part of one's body to another person. Their interviews with kidney donors point to one aspect of the rapprochement between theories of reinforcement and acts of self-sacrifice. In many cases such a sacrifice accrues to the donor's benefit as well—he experiences the inner rewards of increased self-esteem and pride as a consequence of the donation. As one of the donors reported a year after surgery, "I feel I am a better person, much happier than before. . . . I've done something with my life."

The Unresponsive Bystander: Why Doesn't He Help?

Bibb Latané and John M. Darley

Almost 100 years ago, Charles Darwin wrote: "As man is a social animal, it is almost certain that he would . . . from an inherited tendency be willing to defend, in concert with others, his fellow-men; and be ready to aid them in any way, which did not too greatly interfere with his own welfare or his own strong desires" (*The Descent of Man*). Today, although many psychologists would quarrel with Darwin's assertion that altruism is inherited, most would agree that men will go to the aid of others even when there is no visible gain for themselves. At least, most would have agreed until a March night in 1964. That night, Kitty Genovese was set upon by a maniac as she returned home from work at 3:00 A.M. Thirty-eight of her neighbors in Kew Gardens came to their windows when she cried out in terror; but none came to her assistance, even though her stalker took over half an hour to murder her. No one even so much as called the police.

Since we started our research on bystander response to emergencies, we have heard about dozens of such incidents. We have also heard many explanations: "I would assign this to the effect of the megalopolis in which we live, which makes closeness very difficult and leads to the alienation of the individual from the group," contributed a psychoanalyst. "A disaster syndrome," explained a sociologist, "that shook the sense of safety and sureness of the individuals involved and caused psychological withdrawal from the event by ignoring it." "Apathy," others claim. "Indifference." "The gratification of unconscious sadistic impulses." "Lack of concern for our fellow men." "The Cold Society." These explanations and many more have been applied to the surprising failure of bystanders

Abridged from "Social Determinants of Bystander Intervention in Emergencies," in J. Macaulay and L. Berkowitz (Eds.), *Altruism and Helping Behavior*, New York: Academic Press, 1970, pp. 13–27, with permission of the authors and the publisher.

to intervene in emergencies—failures which suggest that we no longer care about the fate of our neighbors.

But can this be so? We think not. Although it is unquestionably true that the witnesses in the incidents above did nothing to save the victim, "apathy," "indifference," and "unconcern" are not entirely accurate descriptions of their reactions. The 38 witnesses of Kitty Genovese's murder did not merely look at the scene once and then ignore it. Instead they continued to stare out of their windows at what was going on. Caught, fascinated, distressed, unwilling to act but unable to turn away, their behavior was neither helpful nor heroic; but it was not indifferent or apathetic either.

Actually, it was like crowd behavior in many other emergency situations; car accidents, drownings, fires, and attempted suicides all attract substantial numbers of people who watch the drama in helpless fascination without getting directly involved in the action. Are these people alienated and indifferent? Are the rest of us? Obviously not. It seems only yesterday we were being called overconforming. But why, then, do we not act?

Paradoxically, the key to understanding these failures of intervention may be found exactly in the fact that so surprises us about them: so many bystanders fail to intervene. If we think of 38, or 11, or 100 individuals, each looking at an emergency and callously deciding to pass by, we are horrified. But if we realize that each bystander is picking up cues about what is happening and how to react to it from the other bystanders, understanding begins to emerge. There are several ways in which a crowd of onlookers can make each individual member of that crowd less likely to act.

DEFINING THE SITUATION

Most emergencies are, or at least begin as, ambiguous events. A quarrel in the street may erupt into violence or it may be simply a family argument. A man staggering about may be suffering a coronary, or an onset of diabetes, or he simply may be drunk. Smoke pouring from a building may signal a fire, but on the other hand, it may be simply steam or air-conditioner vapor. Before a bystander is likely to take action in such ambiguous situations, he must first define the event as an emergency and decide that intervention is the proper course of action.

In the course of making these decisions, it is likely that an individual bystander will be considerably influenced by the decisions he perceives other bystanders to be taking. If everyone else in a group of onlookers seems to regard an event as nonserious and the proper course of action as nonintervention, this consensus may strongly affect the perceptions of any single individual and inhibit his potential intervention.

The definitions that other people hold may be discovered by discussing the situation with them, but they may also be inferred from their facial expressions or behavior. A whistling man with his hands in his pockets obviously does not believe he is in the midst of a crisis. A bystander who does not respond to smoke obviously does not attribute it to fire. An individual, seeing the inaction of others, will judge the situation as less serious then he would if alone.

But why should the others be inactive? Probably because they are aware that other people are also watching them. The others are an audience to their own reactions. Among American males, it is considered desirable to appear poised and collected in times of stress. Being exposed to the public view may constrain the actions and expressions of emotion of any individual as he tries to avoid possible ridicule and embarrassment. Even though he may be truly concerned and upset about the plight of a victim, until he decides what to do, he may maintain a calm demeanor.

If each member of a group is, at the same time, trying to appear calm and also looking around at the other members to gauge their reactions, all members may be led (or misled) by each other to define the situation as less critical than they would if alone. Until someone acts, each person sees only other nonresponding bystanders and is likely to be influenced not to act himself. A state of "pluralistic ignorance" may develop.

It has often been recognized that a crowd can cause contagion of panic, leading each person in the crowd to overreact to an emergency to the detriment of everyone's welfare. What we suggest here is that a crowd can also force inaction on its members. It can suggest by its passive behavior that an event is not to be reacted to as an emergency, and it can make any individual uncomfortably aware of what a fool he will look for behaving as if it is.

WHERE THERE'S SMOKE, THERE'S (SOMETIMES) FIRE[1]

In this experiment we presented an emergency to individuals either alone or in groups of three. It was our expectation that the constraints on behavior in public combined with social influence processes would lessen the likelihood that members of three-person groups would act to cope with the emergency.

College students were invited to an interview to discuss "some of the problems involved in life at an urban university." As they sat in a small room waiting to be called for the interview and filling out a preliminary questionnaire, they faced an ambiguous but potentially dangerous situa-

[1] A more complete account of this experiment is provided in B. Latané and J. M. Darley, "Group inhibition of bystander intervention," *Journal of Personality and Social Psychology*, 1968, **10**, 215–221.

tion. A stream of smoke began to puff into the room through a wall vent.

Some subjects were exposed to this potentially critical situation while alone. In a second condition, three naive subjects were tested together. Since subjects arrived at slightly different times, and since they each had individual questionnaires to work on, they did not introduce themselves to each other or attempt anything but the most rudimentary conversation.

As soon as the subjects had completed two pages of their questionnaires, the experimenter began to introduce the smoke through a small vent in the wall. The "smoke," copied from the famous Camel cigarette sign in Times Square, formed a moderately fine-textured but clearly visible stream of whitish smoke. It continued to jet into the room in irregular puffs, and by the end of the experimental period, it obscured vision.

All behavior and conversation were observed and coded from behind a one-way window (largely disguised on the subject's side by a large sign giving preliminary instructions). When and if the subject left the experimental room and reported the smoke, he was told that the situation "would be taken care of." If the subject had not reported the smoke within 6 minutes from the time he first noticed it, the experiment was terminated.

The typical subject, when tested alone, behaved very reasonably. Usually, shortly after the smoke appeared, he would glance up from his questionnaire, notice the smoke, show a slight but distinct startle reaction, and then undergo a brief period of indecision, perhaps returning briefly to his questionnaire before again staring at the smoke. Soon, most subjects would get up from their chairs, walk over to the vent and investigate it closely, sniffing the smoke, waving their hands in it, feeling its temperature, etc. The usual Alone subject would hesitate again, but finally would walk out of the room, look around outside, and, finding somebody there, calmly report the presence of the smoke. No subject showed any sign of panic, most simply said: "There's something strange going on in there, there seems to be some sort of smoke coming through the wall. . . ." The median subject in the Alone condition had reported the smoke within 2 minutes of first noticing it. Three-quarters of the 24 people run in this condition reported the smoke before the experimental period was terminated.

In contrast, subjects in the three-person-group condition were markedly inhibited from reporting the smoke. In only 38% of the eight groups in this condition did even one person report. Of the 24 people run in these eight groups, only one person reported the smoke within the first 4 minutes before the room got noticeably unpleasant.

The results of this study clearly support the prediction. Groups of three naive subjects were less likely to report the smoke than solitary bystanders. Our predictions were confirmed—but this does not necessarily mean that our explanation of these results is the correct one. Several alternative explanations center around the fact that the smoke represented a possible danger to the subject himself as well as to others in the building. For instance, it is possible that the subjects in groups saw themselves as engaged in a game of "chicken" in which the first person to report would admit his cowardliness. Or it may have been that the presence of others made subjects feel safer, and thus reduced their need to report.

To rule out such explanations, a second experiment was designed to see whether similar group inhibition effects could be observed in situations where there is no danger to the individual himself for not acting. In this study, male Columbia University undergraduates waited either alone or with a stranger to participate in a market research study. As they waited they heard a woman fall and apparently injure herself in the room next door. Whether they tried to help and how long they took to do so were the main dependent variables of the study.

THE FALLEN WOMAN[2]

Subjects were telephoned and offered $2 to participate in a survey of game and puzzle preferences conducted at Columbia by the Consumer Testing Bureau (CTB), a market research organization. When they arrived, they were met at the door by an attractive young woman and taken to the testing room. On the way, they passed the CTB office, and through its open door they were able to see a desk and bookcase piled high with papers and filing cabinets. They entered the adjacent testing room, which contained a table and chairs and a variety of games, and they were given questionnaires to fill out. The representative told subjects that she would be working next door in her office for about 10 minutes while they were completing the questionnaire and left by opening the collapsible curtain which divided the two rooms. She made sure that subjects were aware that the curtain was unlocked and easily opened and that it provided a means of entry to her office. The representative stayed in her office, shuffling papers, opening drawers, and making enough noise to remind the subjects of her presence. Four minutes after leaving the testing area, she turned on a high fidelity stereophonic tape recorder.

THE EMERGENCY

If the subject listened carefully, he heard the representative climb up on a chair to reach for a stack of papers on the bookcase. Even if he were not listening carefully, he heard a loud crash and a scream as the chair collapsed and she fell to the floor. "Oh, my God, my foot . . . I . . . I

[2] This experiment is more fully described in B. Latané and J. Rodin, "A lady in distress: Inhibiting effects of friends and strangers on bystander intervention," *Journal of Experimental Social Psychology*, 1969, 5, 189–202.

. . . can't move . . . it. Oh . . . my ankle," the representative moaned. "I . . . can't get this . . . thing . . . off me." She cried and moaned for about a minute longer, but the cries gradually got more subdued and controlled. Finally she muttered something about getting outside, knocked over the chair as she pulled herself up and thumped to the door, closing it behind her as she left. The entire incident took 130 seconds.

The main dependent variable of the study, of course, was whether the subjects took action to help the victim and how long it took them to do so. There were actually several modes of intervention possible: a subject could open the screen dividing the two rooms, leave the testing room and enter the CTB office by the door, find someone else, or most simply, call out to see if the representative needed help. In one condition, each subject was in the testing room alone while he filled out the questionnaire and heard the fall. In the second condition, strangers were placed in the testing room in pairs. Each subject in the pair was unacquainted with the other before entering the room and they were not introduced.

Since 70% of Alone subjects intervened, we should expect that at least one person in 91% of all two-person groups would offer help if members of a pair had no influence upon each other. In fact, members did influence each other. In only 40% of the groups did even one person offer help to the injured woman. Only eight subjects of the 40 who were run in this condition intervened. Social inhibition of helping was so strong that the victim was actually helped more quickly when only one person heard her distress than when two did.

When we talked to subjects after the experiment, those who intervened usually claimed that they did so either because the fall sounded very serious or because they were uncertain what had occurred and felt they should investigate. Many talked about intervention as the "right thing to do" and asserted they would help again in any situation.

Many of the noninterveners also claimed that they were unsure what had happened (59%), but had decided that it was not too serious (46%). A number of subjects reported that they thought other people would or could help (25%), and three said they refrained out of concern for the victim—they did not want to embarrass her. Whether to accept these explanations as reasons or rationalizations is moot—they certainly do not explain the differences among conditions. The important thing to note is that noninterveners did not seem to feel that they had behaved callously or immorally. Their behavior was generally consistent with their interpretation of the situation. Subjects almost uniformly claimed that in a "real" emergency they would be among the first to help the victim.

Other studies we have done show that group inhibition effects hold in real life as well as in the laboratory, and for members of the general population as well as college students. The results of these experiments clearly support the line of theoretical argument advanced earlier. When bystanders to an emergency can see the reactions of other people, and when other people can see their own reactions, each individual may, through a process of social influence, be led to interpret the situation as less serious than he would if he were alone, and consequently be less likely to take action.

These studies, however, tell us little about the case that stimulated our interest in bystander intervention: the Kitty Genovese murder. Although the 38 witnesses to that event were aware, through seeing lights and silhouettes in other windows, that others watched, they could not see what others were doing and thus be influenced by their reactions. In the privacy of their own apartments, they could not be clearly seen by others, and thus inhibited by their presence. The social influence process we have described above could not operate. Nevertheless, we think that the presence of other bystanders may still have affected each individual's response.

DIFFUSION OF RESPONSIBILITY

In addition to affecting the interpretations that he places on a situation, the presence of other people can also alter the rewards and costs facing an individual bystander. Perhaps most importantly, the presence of other people can reduce the cost of not acting. If only one bystander is present at an emergency, he carries all of the responsibility for dealing with it; he will feel all of the guilt for not acting; he will bear all of any blame others may level for nonintervention. If others are present, the onus of responsibility is diffused, and the individual may be more likely to resolve his conflict between intervening and not intervening in favor of the latter alternative.

When only one bystander is present at an emergency, if help is to come it must be from him. Although he may choose to ignore them out of concern for his personal safety, or desire "not to get involved," any pressures to intervene focus uniquely on him. When there are several observers present, however, the pressures to intervene do not focus on any one of the observers; instead, the responsibility for intervention is shared among all the onlookers and is not unique to any one. As a result, each may be less likely to help.

Potential blame may also be diffused. However much we wish to think that an individual's moral behavior is divorced from considerations of personal punishment or reward, there is both theory and evidence to the contrary. It is perfectly reasonable to assume that under circumstances of group responsibility for a punishable act, the punishment or blame that accrues to any one individual is often slight or nonexistent.

Finally, if others are known to be present, but their behavior cannot be closely observed, any one bystander may assume that one of the other observers is already taking action to end the emergency. If so, his own intervention would only be redundant—perhaps harmfully or confusingly so. Thus, given the presence of other onlookers whose behavior cannot be observed, any given bystander can rationalize his own inaction by convincing himself that "somebody else must be doing something."

These considerations suggest that even when bystanders to an emergency cannot see or be influenced by each other, the more bystanders who are present, the less likely any one bystander would be to intervene and provide aid. To test this suggestion, it would be necessary to create an emergency situation in which each subject is blocked from communicating with others to prevent his getting information about their behavior during the emergency.

A FIT TO BE TRIED[3]

A college student arrived in the laboratory, and was ushered into an individual room from which a communication system would enable him to talk to other participants (who were actually figments of the tape recorder). Over the intercom, the subject was told that the experimenter was concerned with the kinds of personal problems faced by normal college students in a high-pressure, urban environment, and that he would be asked to participate in a discussion about these problems. To avoid embarrassment about discussing personal problems with strangers, the experimenter said, several precautions would be taken. First, subjects would remain anonymous, which was why they had been placed in individual rooms rather than face-to-face. Second, the experimenter would not listen to the initial discussion himself, but would only get the subject's reactions later by questionnaire.

The plan for the discussion was that each person would talk in turn for 2 minutes, presenting his problems to the group. Next, each person in turn would comment on what others had said, and finally there would be a free discussion. A mechanical switching device regulated the discussion, switching on only one microphone at a time.

THE EMERGENCY

The discussion started with the future victim speaking first. He said he found it difficult to get adjusted to New York and to his studies. Very hesitantly and with obvious embarrassment, he mentioned that he was prone to seizures, particularly when studying hard or taking exams. The other people, including the one real subject, took their turns and dis-

[3] Further details of this experiment can be found in J. M. Darley and B. Latané, "Bystander intervention in emergencies: Diffusion of responsibility," *Journal of Personality and Social Psychology* 1968, 8, 377–383.

cussed similar problems (minus the proneness to seizures). The naive subject talked last in the series, after the last prerecorded voice.

When it was again the victim's turn to talk, he made a few relatively calm comments, and then, growing increasingly loud and incoherent, he continued:

I er I think I I need er if if could er er somebody er er er er er er er give me a little er give me a little help here because I er I'm er er h-h-having a a a a real problem er right now and I er if somebody could help me out it would er er s-s-sure be sure be good . . . because er there er er a cause I er I uh I've got a a one of the er sie . . . er er things coming on and and and I could really er use some help so if somebody would er give me a little h-help uh er-er-er-er-er c-could somebody er er help er uh uh uh (choking sounds) . . . . I'm gonna die er er I'm . . . gonna die er help er er seizure (chokes, then quiet).

The major independent variable of the study was the number of people the subject believed also heard the fit. The subject was led to believe that the discussion group was one of three sizes: a two-person group consisting of himself and the victim; a three-person group consisting of himself, the victim and the other person; or a six-person group consisting of himself, the victim, and four other persons.

The major dependent variable of the experiment was the time elapsed from the start of the victim's seizure until the subject left his experimental cubicle. When the subject left his room, he saw the experimental assistant seated at the end of the hall, and invariably went to the assistant to report the seizure. If 5 minutes elapsed without the subject's having emerged from his room, the experiment was terminated.

Eighty-five percent of the subjects who thought they alone knew of the victim's plight reported the seizure before the victim was cut off; only 31% of those who thought four other bystanders were present did so. Every one of the subjects in the two-person condition, but only 62% of the subjects in the six-person condition ever reported the emergency. To do a more detailed analysis of the results, each subject's time score was transformed into a "speed" score by taking the reciprocal of the response time in seconds and multiplying by 100. Analysis of variance of these speed scores indicates that the effect of group size was highly significant, and all three conditions differed significantly from one another.

Subjects, whether or not they intervened, believed the fit to be genuine and serious. "My God, he's having a fit," many subjects said to themselves (and we overheard via their microphones). Others gasped or simply said, "Oh." Several of the male subjects swore. One subject said to herself, "It's just my kind of luck, something has to happen to me!" Several subjects spoke aloud of their confusion about what course of action to take: "Oh, God, what should I do?"

When those subjects who intervened stepped out of their rooms, they found the experimental assistant down the hall. With some uncertainty but without panic, they reported the situation. "Hey, I think Number 1 is very sick. He's having a fit or something." After ostensibly checking on the situation, the experimenter returned to report that "everything is under control." The subjects accepted these assurances with obvious relief.

Subjects who failed to report the emergency showed few signs of the apathy and indifference thought to characterize "unresponsive bystanders." When the experimenter returned to terminate the situation, the subject often asked if the victim was all right. "Is he being taken care of?" "He's all right, isn't he?" Many of these subjects showed physical signs of nervousness; they often had trembling hands and sweating palms. If anything, they seemed more emotionally aroused than did the subjects who reported the emergency.

Why, then, didn't they respond? It is not our impression that they had decided not to respond. Rather, they were still in a state of indecision and conflict concerning whether to respond or not. The emotional behavior of these nonresponding subjects was a sign of their continuing conflict, a conflict that other subjects resolved by responding.

The fit created a conflict situation of the avoidance-avoidance type. On the one hand, subjects worried about the guilt and shame they would feel if they did not help the person in distress. On the other hand, they were concerned not to make fools of themselves by overreacting, not to ruin the ongoing experiment by leaving their intercoms, and not to destroy the anonymous nature of the situation, which the experimenter had earlier stressed as important. For subjects in the two-person condition, the obvious distress of the victim and his need for help were so important that their conflict was easily resolved. For the subjects who knew that there were other bystanders present, the cost of not helping was reduced and the conflict they were in was more acute. Caught between the two negative alternatives of letting the victim continue to suffer or rushing, perhaps foolishly, to help, the nonresponding bystanders vacillated between them rather than choosing not to respond. This distinction may be academic for the victim, since he got no help in either case, but it is an extremely important one for understanding the causes of bystanders' failures to help.

CONCLUSION

We have suggested two distinct processes which might lead people to be less likely to intervene in an emergency if there are other people present than if they are alone. First, we suggested that the presence of other people may affect the interpretations each bystander puts on an ambiguous emergency situation. If other people are present at an emergency, each bystander will be guided by their apparent reactions in formulating his own impressions. Unfortunately, their apparent reactions may not be a good indication of their true feelings. It is possible for a state of "pluralistic ignorance" to develop, in which each bystander is led by the apparent lack of concern of the others to interpret the situation as being less serious than he would if alone. To the extent that he does not feel the situation is an emergency, he will be unlikely to take any helpful action.

Second, even if an individual does decide that there is an emergency and that something ought to be done, he still is faced with the choice of whether or not to intervene. Here again, the presence of other people may influence him—by reducing the costs associated with nonintervention. If a number of people witness the same event, the responsibility for action is diffused, and each may feel less necessity to help.

"There's safety in numbers," according to an old adage, and modern city dwellers seem to believe it. They shun deserted streets, empty subway cars, and lonely dark walks in dark parks, preferring instead to go where others are or to stay at home. When faced with stress, most individuals seem less afraid when they are in the presence of others than when they are alone. But whereas it is certainly true that a victim is unlikely to receive help if nobody knows of his plight, the experiments above cast doubt on the suggestion that he will be more likely to receive help if more people are present. In fact, the opposite seems to be true. A victim may be more likely to get help, or an emergency to be reported, the fewer the people who are available to take action.

Although the results of these studies may shake our faith in "safety in numbers," they also may help us begin to understand a number of frightening incidents where crowds have heard but not answered a call for help. Newspapers have tagged these incidents with the label, "apathy." We have become indifferent, they say, callous to the fate or suffering of others. Our society has become "dehumanized" as it has become urbanized. These glib phrases may contain some truth, since startling cases such as the Genovese murder often seem to occur in our large cities, but such terms may also be misleading. Our studies suggest a different conclusion. They suggest that situational factors, specifically factors involving the immediate social environment, may be of greater importance in determining an individual's reaction to an emergency than such vague cultural or personality concepts as "apathy" or "alienation due to urbanization." They suggest that the failure to intervene may be better understood by knowing the relationship among bystanders rather than that between a bystander and the victim.

* * *

For a complete account of this research, see Bibb Latané and John M. Darley, *The Unresponsive Bystander: Why Doesn't He Help* (New York: Appleton-Century-Crofts, 1970).

Kidney Donors

Carl H. Fellner and John R. Marshall

The first renal homotransplantation was performed in 1936, but only in the last few years have we ceased to think of it as a clearly experimental procedure, and by now more than a thousand human kidney transplants have been performed (60% from living donors). The spectacular progress in human organ transplantation in general has spurred public debate of the moral and ethical aspects of human donorship. Aside from donor physical considerations or those having to do with donor–recipient suitability, it is also the physician's responsibility to protect the donor's right and welfare. The donor must be made fully aware of the many risks he is accepting and of the possibility that his sacrifice may be of little benefit to the recipient ("informed consent"). The donation must be entirely voluntary, free from undue pressure, and must come from a "genuine volunteer."

In the spirit of this concern for the safeguarding of the donor's rights and welfare, we were approached by the renal transplantation team of our hospital to participate in a routine psychiatric screening of all possible donors. Before acceding to such an extensive obligation, however, we undertook to study all available previous donors to find out how they had become involved, how they had made their decisions, what surgery had meant to them, and how they have fared since. We interviewed some thirty donors or potential donors, either before or after surgery. It was made clear at the beginning of each interview that all information was confidential and only general conclusions would ultimately be discussed with the renal team. There were six mothers and one father among those interviewed. The rest were siblings.

The medical selection procedure adopted by the renal transplantation team is as follows: When a transplant situation arises, all possible donor

Abridged from J. Macaulay and L. Berkowitz (Eds.), *Altruism and Helping Behavior*, New York: Academic Press, 1970, pp. 269–281, with permission of the authors and the publisher.

relatives are asked to come to the clinic for blood tests (ABO typing). Great care is taken at this point by the medical staff to inform the volunteer subjects that this is an exceedingly preliminary procedure, and that no commitment whatsover is involved by their appearing at this clinic, or elsewhere, to have blood samples drawn. Those potential donors who are not ruled out on the basis of blood grouping are then asked to take part in an extensive series of medical examinations, making it possible for the transplant team to select from among the available possible donors the most suitable one. Only at the end of this evaluation and after intensive, repeated briefing on the risks involved and of the chances for success, is the potential donor asked to make a decision, and permitted, if he so desires, to give his informed consent. A final chance to refuse in a dignified and comfortable manner is offered in the team's expressed willingness to supply a plausible medical excuse to the recipient and family.

FINDINGS

In our interviews with the donors we tried to follow events and reactions chronologically from the moment of first communication about renal transplant, through the selection process, decision making, surgery, post-surgical phase, to the interview with us.

COMMUNICATION

Only one donor had first heard of the transplant possibility from a member of the renal transplant team. Three had heard directly from the recipient, nine from the recipient's spouse, five from their mother, and two had been told by the family physician prior to the transfer of the patient to our hospital. Usually, communication was by telephone call in which the future donor was told about the seriousness of the future recipient's illness, that the doctors were considering a kidney transplantation, and that all close relatives would be invited in the near future to come to the clinic for some blood tests. Usually, the informant followed this up with a brief discussion of who from among the other family members should be asked to participate, and who should not, and for what reasons. The same route of communication was subsequently used to transmit the results of tests and make further appointments.

DECISION MAKING

At what point in the long process that followed the initial contact with the potential donor did he actually make his decision? Did he hold off, seek information, consider the facts, and make an informed decision at the end, when all studies were completed and he was asked by the doctors to give his informed consent?

Actually, most of the members of the renal transplant team were aware that most donors were ready to make a commitment earlier than that and had to be held off until the team had made its selection. It was thought that the point of commitment to the procedure was reached about halfway through the medical evaluation process.

Our findings were, therefore, surprising. It appeared that not one of the donors weighed the alternatives and decided rationally. Fourteen of the donors and five of the prospective donors waiting for surgery stated that they made their decision immediately when the subject of the kidney transplant was first mentioned over the telephone—"in a split second," "instantaneously," "right away." Five said they just went along with the tests hoping it would be someone else. They could not recall ever really having made a clear decision, yet they never considered refusing to go along either, and as it became clear toward the end of the selection process that they were going to be the person most suited to be the donor, they finally committed themselves to the act. However, this decision, too, still occurred before the session with the team doctors in which all the relevant information and statistics were put before them and they were finally asked to decide.

POSTDECISION PERIOD

Once the decision had been made by the prospective donor, he carefully refrained from considering further data and engaged in several maneuvers which permitted him never to vary in his decision or even to question it.[1] For example, nine of the donors felt immediately convinced that in the end, after all of the tests had been done, they would be the ones to be chosen and they never wavered in this conviction. Two were less convinced but hoped very strongly to become the chosen ones. Three had initially equally strong convictions that it would be someone else and not they (these were the three donors who had not made an initial decision but had gone along with the tests until the other possible donors had been eliminated). Of the 19 subjects who, as mentioned earlier, made their decision on the telephone on first hearing of the possibility of the kidney transplant, none had consulted his spouse. When questioned about this particular circumstance they all explained that the spouse later on had

[1] For discussions of such postdecision processes, see K. Lewin, in D. Cartwright (Ed.), *Field Theory in Social Science: Selected Theoretical Papers* (New York: Harper, 1951); L. Festinger, *A Theory of Cognitive Dissonance* (Stanford, Calif.: Stanford University Press, 1957); and L. Festinger, *Conflict, Decision and Dissonance* (Stanford, Calif.: Stanford University Press, 1964).

either been neutral or reinforced their decision. To the hypothetical question of: "What would you have done if your spouse had said no?" they all answered: "I would have gone ahead and done it anyway." Several of the donors volunteered the information that friends and acquaintances had tried to dissuade them but, as one of them put it, "They might as well have been talking to a brick wall."

Another way in which the original decision was being maintained could be seen in the viewing of the rigorous medical examinations as an achievement test which, if passed, entitled the prospective donor to contribute his kidney. Some comments were "Those were tough tests, but I passed," or "It's good to know you are the healthiest of the bunch," or "The doctors would never let me do it unless I were in perfect condition."

For some of the chosen donors, the time of the initial testing and gradual elimination of the other potential donors was quite stressful and they reported feeling greatly relieved and, in some cases, even elated when they were told of the final decision: "I was glad they told me; the suspense is over." "I was relieved when I was told it was me; I feel good that someone could for sure." "When informed I felt elated that it would be me; it was just a good feeling."

With regard to the instructions and explanations offered repeatedly by the doctors of the renal transplant team in an attempt to provide the basis for an informed consent, the donors all reported that they had not really been very curious or interested in what the doctors were telling them. Almost uniformly, this information was used in exactly the opposite way to that which was intended. The prospective donors reasoned in the following manner: All of the doctors are making an effort to tell me the bad possibilities, which means that they must be honest and therefore capable and I can place my life in their hands without any danger. One donor said: "What the doctors said went in one ear and out the other." She was content to leave the details to the doctors: "They know what they're doing."

THE FAMILY SYSTEM OF DONOR SELECTION

In addition to the medical selection system and the donor self-selection described, we believe that there is a third, or family, system of selection in operation. This is rather difficult to demonstrate but, in retrospect, it seems possible that the difficulty arises from the general expectation, which we initially shared, that the family would tend to select a likely donor in the sense of a sacrifice or scapegoat under threat of family ostracism. We could never demonstrate this in our sample, except perhaps in one rather questionable case. What we finally came to see was that a family would *exclude* certain members from participation. This was done most commonly at the time of the initial contact. In one family, the father successfully dissuaded his two sons from even coming for the preliminary blood tests, and his wife from participating beyond the halfway point, and ended up as the triumphant donor himself. In another family, the mother tried very hard to beat out her son in competition for donorship, but lost. One woman, who became the donor for her son, had never mentioned that the father of the recipient, from whom she had been divorced years earlier, was alive and well. One donor who gave up a kidney for his brother explained afterwards that the family decided not to call upon the grown son of the recipient since there was bad blood between father and son over the divorce of the father and mother.

THE POSTOPERATIVE PERIOD

Kemph[2] has described a period of depression beginning 3–5 days after surgery and lasting for varying lengths of time. Brief supportive psychotherapy was clearly required in every case. It was Kemph's interpretation that the donors felt depressed and unrewarded for a maximal sacrifice, and resentful of the much greater amount of attention shown to the recipient.

Our own findings, based on the self-report by the donors plus a review of the hospital charts and discussion with the renal team who followed these patients, did not reveal any evidence of the depressive reactions observed by Kemph. None of our subjects had feelings of being neglected or treated less well than the recipient, and only a few had mild and short-lived depressive reactions.

The comment is often made that donors "give up something and get nothing in return." This is a frequent theme in discussions on the ethics of organ transplants in general. The postoperative depression is related to this by some authors, but usually the general unfairness of this exchange is quoted without further substantiation. By contrast, all of our donors reported that this had been a very meaningful experience in their lives, of substantial impact on them, and that it had brought about changes in them which they felt were beneficial. There appeared to be two overlapping phases to this experience. The first began just prior to and continued through the immediate postoperative period, usually a month or two. During this phase they received a good deal of attention about their sacrifice either by word of mouth or through the local news-from their families and friends and also from strangers who had heard papers.

Our subjects were rather hesitant to talk about this attention out of a

[2] J. P. Kemph, "Renal failure, artificial kidney and kidney transplant," *American Journal of Psychiatry*, 1966, *122*, 1270–1274; and "Psychotherapy with patients receiving kidney transplant," *American Journal of Psychiatry*, 1967, *124*, 623–629.

sense of modesty but seemed relieved when we gave them the opportunity to verbalize their feelings and share them with us.

They related how this attention made them feel "good," "noble," "bigger," "happier," and generally increased their self-esteem. They all added, some with disappointment, that this attention rapidly diminished and they soon ceased to be celebrities. It was at this point, later, that they noted certain changes in their attitudes or ideas of themselves which they considered more lasting. The following are representative quotations:

(A 30-year-old female donor, 12 months postoperatively.) I have much more confidence; before, I was more afraid of what people would say . . . . I feel I am a better person, much happier than before. . . . The whole of my life is different. I've done something with my life.

(A 25-year-old female donor, 3 months postoperatively.) I am a better church goer, we think of it as a miracle . . . . I take things more seriously now. I am careful to lead a good life, perhaps I'll be rewarded later. I was a real snot; I feel I was chosen, to teach me. Now I think of others more. My marriage is better, closer now. I was lucky for the opportunity.

(A 40-year-old male donor, 4 weeks postoperatively.) I feel better, kind of noble. I am changed. I have passed a milestone in my life, more confidence, self-esteem . . . . In every way I am better. For realizing how far I could go for others, I am up a notch in life . . . . I value things more, big and small things . . . . I come in contact with others a bit more. My pleasures are bigger and have more meaning.

(A 31-year-old female donor, 15 months postoperatively.) I have done a lot of growing up as a result of this. I am much more responsible. People say I act older . . . . It gives me inner satisfaction. When I have moments of depression, I think of my sister. I am happy.

(A 38-year-old female donor, 8 months postoperatively.) I keep thinking how fast it all was and I plan for now rather than the future. We are taking a trip this summer I have been putting off . . . . I changed, things are more trivial now. I do feel good but more mortal now.

(A 59-year-old female donor, 18 months postoperatively.) I feel I am a better person for having done it, more understanding, not nearly as critical. I have improved in many ways, even am more respectful of myself as a person. I feel, if I can do this, I can do anything.

One 31-year-old male donor who had undergone considerable life-saving surgery in his childhood said: "I had always wondered whether God had been saving me for something. I knew from the beginning that this was it; it balances things out. I feel bigger now, a better person. It's time I got something out of it. I'm not going to work as hard or be as compulsive. I'm going to enjoy life more now. I'm aged and wiser now. Somehow more considerate and tolerant." One donor who had been on leave from the service for the purpose of donating his kidney said: "I had never done anything like it before. I have always been drifting along with the tide and this is the first time I did something worthwhile. I felt good whilst I was up here; felt more optimistic towards life at first and about my own potential but when I got back to base I got into a rut again; all seemed to stop. The service has done something to me."

When the subjects were asked to compare the act of having donated a kidney to any other act in their lives of equal importance or consequence, most of them could not do so. One of the subjects did compare it to volunteering for a dangerous mission during the Korean War: disarming an unexploded bomb to save the lives of his comrades. A female donor compared it to giving birth to a child. Another female donor compared it to having once saved a child from drowning when she was 16 or 17, but quickly added that it did not really compare in intensity and effect. None of the others could come up with comparable events or actions in their own previous lives and likened their action to a feat of heroism that "ordinary life just doesn't give a person a chance for." There were two exceptions to this particular feeling: two mothers who had donated their kidneys to a son seemed to feel, as one of them put it, "Something had to be done and mothers do more for their children ordinarily anyway. It was not such a big thing."

In addition to describing their own personal gain in terms of increased self-esteem, etc., several of the donors also remarked that the whole family had somehow changed for the better, had become closer, was drawn more together and emerged with a new and positive feeling of unity as a result of the kidney transplantation.

COMMENT

It is possible that these increases in self-esteem are temporary changes which will diminish as time passes. But we think not, since we interviewed several of these donors more than a year after surgery. If this finding is as extensive as our small sample would indicate, then the prevalent idea that the donor "gives something but receives nothing in return" should be reexamined.

We felt a plausible explanation might be derived from crisis theory:

> Crisis involves a relatively short period of psychological disequilibrium in a person who confronts a hazardous circumstance that for him constitutes an important problem which he can for the time being neither escape nor solve with his customary problem-solving resources. During the upset, the individual works out a novel way of handling the problem through new sources of strength in himself and his environment. The upset then abates, and he returns to psychological equilibrium and consistent behavior.[3]

The new pattern may differ from the previous one and become stable, since it is then maintained as the new equilibrium.

[3] G. Caplan, *Principles of Preventive Psychiatry* (New York: Basic Books, 1964), p. 53.

This kind of phenomenon may have occurred in our donors. A post-crisis equilibrium can move in a positive or in a negative direction (in other words, beneficial or harmful life-style changes), and Caplan further points out how the direction of resolution may be influenced by the resources present either internally or externally. We saw no indication of detrimental feelings or attitudes related to the surgery. The forces on the donors in a positive direction came from several sources: (*a*) their belief in the "good" they were doing for the recipient, saving a life, (*b*) their positive relationship with their physician, both actual and symbolically, (*c*) the positive emotional reinforcement from the recipient and family, and (*d*) the considerable attention paid to them by friends, acquaintances, news media, etc.

Actually, we should not be surprised that an act of altruism such as this can and does have far-reaching positive effects in the life of a person. After all, it is in keeping with the highest ideals of our society, in a time and age which does not offer much opportunity for public acts of courage and devotion in which one can transcend oneself. We found that for our group of donors, their action had provided them with a peak experience, or as Maslow says, an experience in which "the IS and OUGHT merge with each other instead of being different and contradictory," and which "can be considered to be truly a religious experience in the best and most profound, most universal, and most humanistic sense of the word." [4]

CONCLUSION

As far as we could ascertain from our sample, the concept of "informed consent" is just another myth. We would interpret this to mean that the physician's responsibility to safeguard the rights and interests of the donor go even further than heretofore conceptualized. However, in weighing the "pros and cons" for a potential donor, we must also be very much aware that to give a kidney is not solely a liability but can become a turning point, a peak experience of considerable positive impact on the overall life development of the donor.

[4] A. H. Maslow, "Lessons from the peak-experiences," *Journal of Humanistic Psychology,* 1962, *2,* 9–18.

LOVING

Loving has probably been talked about more and studied less than any other aspect of human behavior. In his presidential address to the American Psychological Association in 1956, Theodore M. Newcomb lamented the fact that psychologists, like their lay contemporaries, had assumed that the matters of liking and loving were "altogether too ineffable" to be topics of systematic research. In another presidential address to the same organization two years later, Harry F. Harlow bluntly concluded: "So far as love or affection is concerned, psychologists have failed in their mission. The little we know about love does not transcend simple observation and the little we write about it has been written better by poets and novelists." In the years since these statements were made, however, social scientists have begun to apply scientific tools to penetrate the mysteries of love. These initial investigations demonstrate, moreover, that love is not an entity totally unto itself, but rather an element of social life that is closely integrated with the other elements that we have been considering.

Love may take place in many contexts, including parent-child, same-sex, and opposite-sex relationships. However, the three papers included in this section all focus on what may be broadly categorized as "romantic love"—that is, the sort of love that may exist between opposite-sex partners.

William J. Goode stresses the integration of love with other aspects of social life in his analysis of "the theoretical importance of love." Viewing the matter from a sociological vantage point, he notes that to the extent that love can cross class lines, it threatens to disrupt social arrangements. As he puts it, "To permit random mating would mean radical change in the social structure." To deal with this threat, all societies have devised means of insuring that love arises only between "appropriate" pairs. In some societies such direct means of control as arranged marriage are employed. Our own society makes use of more subtle means of control, relying on processes of molding such as those considered in previous sections.

One aspect of this molding is the way in which young men and women are taught to identify particular experiences or events as "love." Elaine Walster presents a detailed analysis of the falling-in-love process, based on a more general social-psychological theory of emotion. This theory, which was first propounded by Stanley Schachter, holds that the experience of any given emotion involves two separate stages. The first is the experience of physiological arousal (e.g., a quickened breath, a beating heart), and the second is the labeling of the arousal as a particular emotion, such as "anger," "fear," or "love." The rules for this labeling are learned from other people, both directly and through the mass media. This approach to love can be seen as a direct extension of Schachter's earlier work on the psychology of affiliation. We join other people in order to find out how we really feel, and what we learn from others in fact has an impact on our own feelings.

In my own research, romantic love has been viewed as an interpersonal attitude—that is, a cluster of feelings, thoughts, and behavioral predispositions held by one person toward a particular other. I have attempted to measure this attitude, and to assess its links with other attitudes and behaviors. My definition of love includes components of both attachment and caring. Attachment is marked by a desire to be in the other person's presence, and directly reflects the theme of joining (especially as approached by Robert S. Weiss). Caring involves the concern for another person's well-being, and thus reflects the theme of helping (as revealed especially in Fellner and Marshall's paper on kidney donors). In a sense, then, loving may be viewed as one of the most encompassing ways of doing unto others, including and recreating a variety of other patterns.

The Theoretical Importance of Love

William J. Goode

Because love often determines the intensity of an attraction[1] toward or away from an intimate relationship with another person, it can become one element in a decision or action.[2] Nevertheless, serious sociological attention has only infrequently been given to love. Moreover, analyses of love generally have been confined to mate choice in the Western World, while the structural importance of love has been for the most part ignored. The present paper views love in a broad perspective, focusing on the structural patterns by which societies keep in check the potentially disruptive effect of love relationships on mate choice and stratification systems.

TYPES OF LITERATURE ON LOVE

For obvious reasons, the printed material on love is immense. For our present purposes, it may be classified as follows:

1. Poetic, humanistic, literary, erotic, pornographic: By far the largest body of all literature on love views it as a sweeping experience. The poet

---

Reprinted from the *American Sociological Review,* 1959, *24,* 38–47, with permission of the author and the American Sociological Association. This paper was completed under a grant (No. M-2526-S) by the National Institute of Mental Health.

[1] On the psychological level, the motivational power of both love and sex is intensified by this curious fact (which I have not seen remarked on elsewhere): Love is the most projective of emotions, as sex is the most projective of drives; only with great difficulty can the attracted person believe that the object of his love or passion does not and will not reciprocate the feeling at all. Thus, the person may carry his action quite far, before accepting a rejection as genuine.

[2] I have treated decision analysis extensively in an unpublished paper by that title.

arouses our sympathy and empathy. The essayist enjoys, and asks the reader to enjoy, the interplay of people in love. The storyteller—Boccaccio, Chaucer, Dante—pulls back the curtain of human souls and lets the reader watch the intimate lives of others caught in an emotion we all know. Others—Vatsyayana, Ovid, William IX Count of Poitiers and Duke of Aquitaine, Marie de France, Andreas Capellanus—have written how-to-do-it books, that is, how to conduct oneself in love relations, to persuade others to succumb to one's love wishes, or to excite and satisfy one's sex partner.[3]

2. Marital counseling: Many modern sociologists have commented on the importance of romantic love in America and its lesser importance in other societies, and have disparaged it as a poor basis for marriage, or as immaturity. Perhaps the best known of these arguments are those of Ernest R. Mowrer, Ernest W. Burgess, Mabel A. Elliott, Andrew G. Truxal, Francis E. Merrill, and Ernest R. Groves.[4] The antithesis of romantic love, in such analyses, is "conjugal" love; the love between a settled, domestic couple.

A few sociologists, remaining within this same evaluative context, have instead claimed that love also has salutary effects in our society. Thus, for example, William L. Kolb[5] has tried to demonstrate that the marital counselors who attack romantic love are really attacking some fundamental values of our larger society, such as individualism, freedom, and personality growth. Beigel[6] has argued that if the female is sexually repressed, only the psychotherapist or love can help her overcome her inhibitions. He claims further that one influence of love in our society is that it extenuates illicit sexual relations; he goes on to assert: "Seen in proper perspective, [love] has not only done no harm as a prerequisite to marriage, but it has mitigated the impact that a too-fast-moving and

[3] Vatsyayana, *The Kama Sutra,* Delhi: Rajkamal, 1948; Ovid, "The Loves," and "Remedies of Love," in *The Art of Love,* Cambridge, Mass.: Harvard University Press, 1939; Andreas Capellanus, *The Art of Courtly Love,* translated by John J. Parry, New York: Columbia University Press, 1941; Paul Tuffrau, editor, *Marie de France: Les Lais de Marie de France,* Paris L'edition d'art, 1925; see also Julian Harris, *Marie de France,* New York: Institute of French Studies, 1930, esp. Chapter 3. All authors but the first *also* had the goal of writing literature.

[4] Ernest R. Mowrer, *Family Disorganization,* Chicago: The University of Chicago Press, 1927, pp. 158–165; Ernest W. Burgess and Harvey J. Locke, *The Family,* New York: American Book, 1953, pp. 436–437; Mabel A. Elliott and Francis E. Merrill, *Social Disorganization,* New York: Harper, 1950, pp. 366–384; Andrew G. Truxal and Francis E. Merrill, *The Family in American Culture,* New York: Prentice-Hall, 1947, pp. 120–124, 507–509; Ernest R. Groves and Gladys Hoagland Groves, *The Contemporary American Family,* New York: Lippincott, 1947, pp. 321–324.

[5] William L. Kolb, "Sociologically Established Norms and Democratic Values," *Social Forces,* 26 (May, 1948), pp. 451–456.

[6] Hugo G. Beigel, "Romantic Love," *American Sociological Review,* 16 (June, 1951), pp. 326–334.

unorganized conversion to new socio-economic constellations has had upon our whole culture and it has saved monogamous marriage from complete disorganization."

In addition, there is widespread comment among marriage analysts, that in a rootless society, with few common bases for companionship, romantic love holds a couple together long enough to allow them to begin marriage. That is, it functions to attract people powerfully together, and to hold them through the difficult first months of the marriage, when their different backgrounds would otherwise make an adjustment troublesome.

3. Although the writers cited above concede the structural importance of love implicitly, since they are arguing that it is either harmful or helpful to various values and goals of our society, a third group has given explicit if unsystematic attention to its structural importance. Here, most of the available propositions point to the functions of love, but a few deal with the conditions under which love relationships occur. They include:

(1) An implicit or assumed descriptive proposition is that love as a common prelude to and basis of marriage is rare, perhaps to be found as a pattern only in the United States.

(2) Most explanations of the conditions which create love are psychological, stemming from Freud's notion that love is "aim-inhibited sex." [7] This idea is expressed, for example, by Waller who says that love is an idealized passion which develops from the frustration of sex.[8] This proposition, although rather crudely stated and incorrect as a general explanation, is widely accepted.

(3) Of course, a predisposition to love is created by the socialization experience. Thus some textbooks on the family devote extended discussion to the ways in which our society socializes for love. The child, for example, is told that he or she will grow up to fall in love with some one, and early attempts are made to pair the child with children of the opposite sex. There is much joshing of children about falling in love; myths and stories about love and courtship are heard by children; and so on.

(4) A further proposition (the source of which I have not been able to locate) is that, in a society in which a very close attachment between parent and child prevails, a love complex is necessary in order to motivate the child to free him from his attachment to his parents.

(5) Love is also described as one final or crystallizing element in the decision to marry, which is otherwise structured by factors such as class, ethnic origin, religion, education, and residence.

(6) Parsons has suggested three factors which "underlie the prominence of the romantic context in our culture": (a) the youth culture frees the individual from family attachments, thus permitting him to fall in love; (b) love is a substitute for the interlocking of kinship roles found in other societies, and

[7] Sigmund Freud, *Group Psychology and the Analysis of the Ego,* London: Hogarth, 1922, p. 72.

[8] Willard Waller, *The Family,* New York: Dryden, 1938, pp. 189–192.

thus motivates the individual to conform to proper marital role behavior; and (c) the structural isolation of the family so frees the married partners' affective inclinations that they are able to love one another.[9]

(7) Robert F. Winch has developed a theory of "complementary needs" which essentially states that the underlying dynamic in the process of falling in love is an interaction between (a) the perceived psychological attributes of one individual and (b) the complementary psychological attributes of the person falling in love, such that the needs of the latter are felt to be met by the perceived attributes of the former and *vice versa.* These needs are derived from Murray's list of personality characteristics. Winch thus does not attempt to solve the problem of why our society has a love complex, but how it is that specific individuals fall in love with each other rather than with someone else.[10]

(8) Winch and others have also analyzed the effect of love upon various institutions or social patterns: Love themes are prominently displayed in the media of entertainment and communication, in consumption patterns, and so on.[11]

4. Finally, there is the cross-cultural work of anthropologists, who in the main have ignored love as a factor of importance in kinship patterns. The implicit understanding seems to be that love as a pattern is found only in the United States, although of course individual cases of love are sometimes recorded. The term "love" is practically never found in indexes of anthropological monographs on specific societies or in general anthropology textbooks. It is perhaps not an exaggeration to say that Lowie's comment of a generation ago would still be accepted by a substantial number of anthropologists:

> But of love among savages? . . . Passion, of course, is taken for granted; affection, which many travelers vouch for, might be conceded; but Love? Well, the romantic sentiment occurs in simpler conditions, as with us—in fiction. . . . So Love exists for the savage as it does for ourselves—in adolescence, in fiction, among the poetically minded.[12]

A still more skeptical opinion is Linton's scathing sneer:

> All societies recognize that there are occasional violent, emotional attachments between persons of opposite sex, but our present American culture is practically the only one which has attempted to capitalize these, and make them the basis for marriage. . . . The hero of the modern American movie is always a romantic lover, just as the hero of the old Arab epic is always an epileptic. A cynic may suspect that in any ordinary population the percentage of individuals with a

9 Talcott Parsons, *Essays in Sociological Theory,* Glencoe, Ill.: Free Press, 1949, pp. 187–189.

10 Robert F. Winch, *Mate Selection,* New York: Harper, 1958.

11 See, e.g., Robert F. Winch, *The Modern Family,* New York: Holt, 1952, Chapter 14.

12 Robert H. Lowie, "Sex and Marriage," in John F. McDermott, editor, *The Sex Problem in Modern Society,* New York: Modern Library, 1931, p. 146.

capacity for romantic love of the Hollywood type was about as large as that of persons able to throw genuine epileptic fits.[13]

In Murdock's book on kinship and marriage, there is almost no mention, if any, of love.[14] Should we therefore conclude that, cross-culturally, love is not important, and thus cannot be of great importance structurally? If there is only one significant case, perhaps it is safe to view love as generally unimportant in social structure and to concentrate rather on the nature and functions of romantic love within the Western societies in which love is obviously prevalent. As brought out below, however, many anthropologists have in fact described love *patterns.* And one of them, Max Gluckman,[15] has recently subsumed a wide range of observations under the broad principle that love relationships between husband and wife estrange the couple from their kin, who therefore try in various ways to undermine that love. This principle is applicable to many more societies (for example, China and India) than Gluckman himself discusses.

THE PROBLEM AND ITS CONCEPTUAL CLARIFICATION

The preceding propositions (except those denying that love is distributed widely) can be grouped under two main questions: What are the consequences of romantic love in the United States? How is the emotion of love aroused or created in our society? The present paper deals with the first question. For theoretical purposes both questions must be reformulated, however, since they implicitly refer only to our peculiar system of romantic love. Thus: (1) In what ways do various love patterns fit into the social structure, especially into the systems of mate choice and stratification? (2) What are the structural conditions under which a range of love patterns occurs in various societies? These are overlapping questions, but their starting point and assumptions are different. The first assumes that love relationships are a universal psychosocial possibility, and that different social systems make different adjustments to their potential disruptiveness. The second does not take love for granted, and supposes rather that such relationships will be rare unless certain structural factors are present. Since in both cases the analysis need not depend upon the correctness of the assumption, the problem may be chosen arbitrarily. Let us begin with the first.[16]

[13] Ralph Linton, *The Study of Man,* New York: Appleton-Century, 1936, p. 175.

[14] George Peter Murdock, *Social Structure,* New York: Macmillan, 1949.

[15] Max Gluckman, *Custom and Conflict in Africa,* Oxford: Basil Blackwell, 1955, Chapter 3.

[16] I hope to deal with the second problem in another paper.

We face at once the problem of defining "love." Here, love is defined as a strong emotional attachment, a cathexis, between adolescents or adults of opposite sexes, with at least the components of sex desire and tenderness. Verbal definitions of this emotional relationship are notoriously open to attack; this one is no more likely to satisfy critics than others. Agreement is made difficult by value judgments: one critic would exclude anything but "true" love, another casts out "infatuation," another objects to "puppy love," while others would separate sex desire from love because sex presumably is degrading. Nevertheless, most of us have had the experience of love, just as we have been greedy, or melancholy, or moved by hate (defining "true" hate seems not to be a problem). The experience can be referred to without great ambiguity, and a refined measure of various degrees of intensity or purity of love is unnecessary for the aims of the present analysis.

Since love may be related in diverse ways to the social structure, it is necessary to forego the dichotomy of "romantic love—no romantic love" in favor of a continuum or range between polar types. At one pole, a strong love attraction is socially viewed as a laughable or tragic aberration; at the other, it is mildly shameful to marry without being in love with one's intended spouse. This is a gradation from negative sanction to positive approval, ranging at the same time from low or almost nonexistent institutionalization of love to high institutionalization.

The urban middle classes of contemporary Western society, especially in the United States, are found toward the latter pole. Japan and China, in spite of the important movement toward European patterns, fall toward the pole of low institutionalization. Village and urban India is farther toward the center, for there the ideal relationship has been one which at least generated love after marriage, and sometimes after betrothal, in contrast with the mere respect owed between Japanese and Chinese spouses.[17] Greece after Alexander, Rome of the Empire, and perhaps the later period of the Roman Republic as well, are near the center, but somewhat toward the pole of institutionalization, for love matches appear to have increased in frequency—a trend denounced by moralists.[18]

This conceptual continuum helps to clarify our problem and to interpret the propositions reviewed above. Thus it may be noted, first, that in-

[17] Tribal India, of course, is too heterogeneous to place in any one position on such a continuum. The question would have to be answered for each tribe. Obviously it is of less importance here whether China and Japan, in recent decades, have moved "two points over" toward the opposite pole of high approval of love relationships as a basis for marriage than that both systems as classically described viewed love as generally a tragedy; and love was supposed to be irrelevant to marriage, i.e., noninstitutionalized. The continuum permits us to place a system at some position, once we have the descriptive data.

[18] See Ludwig Friedländer, *Roman Life and Manners under the Early Empire* (Seventh Edition), translated by A. Magnus, New York: Dutton, 1908, Vol. 1, Chapter 5, "The Position of Women."

dividual love relationships may occur even in societies in which love is viewed as irrelevant to mate choice and excluded from the decision to marry. As Linton conceded, some violent love attachments may be found in any society. In our own, the Song of Solomon, Jacob's love of Rachel, and Michal's love for David are classic tales. The Mahabharata, the great Indian epic, includes love themes. Romantic love appears early in Japanese literature, and the use of Mt. Fuji as a locale for the suicide of star crossed lovers is not a myth invented by editors of tabloids. There is the familiar tragic Chinese story to be found on the traditional "willowplate," with its lovers transformed into doves. And so it goes—individual love relationships seem to occur everywhere. But this fact does not change the position of a society on the continuum.

Second, reading both Linton's and Lowie's comments in this new conceptual context reduces their theoretical importance, for they are both merely saying that people do not *live by* the romantic complex, here or anywhere else. Some few couples in love will brave social pressures, physical dangers, or the gods themselves, but nowhere is this usual. Violent, self-sufficient love is not common anywhere. In this respect, of course, the U.S. is not set apart from other systems.

Third, we can separate a *love pattern* from the romantic love *complex*. Under the former, love is a permissible, expected prelude to marriage, and a usual element of courtship—thus, at about the center of the continuum, but toward the pole of institutionalization. The romantic love complex (one pole of the continuum) includes, in addition, an ideological prescription that falling in love is a highly desirable basis of courtship and marriage; love is strongly institutionalized.[19] In contemporary United States, many individuals would even claim that entering marriage without being in love requires some such rationalization as asserting that one is too old for such romances or that one must "think of practical matters like money." To be sure, both anthropologists and sociologists often exaggerate the American commitment to romance;[20] nevertheless, a behavioral and value complex of this type is found here.

[19] For a discussion of the relation between behavior patterns and the process of institutionalization, see my *After Divorce,* Glencoe, Ill.: Free Press, 1956, Chapter 15.

[20] See Ernest W. Burgess and Paul W. Wallin, *Engagement and Marriage,* New York: Lippincott, 1953, Chapter 7 for the extent to which even the engaged are not blind to the defects of their beloveds. No one has ascertained the degree to which various age and sex groups in our society actually believe in some form of the ideology.

Similarly, Margaret Mead in *Coming of Age in Samoa,* New York: Modern Library, 1953, rates Manu'an love as shallow, and though these Samoans give much attention to love-making, she asserts that they laughed with incredulous contempt at Romeo and Juliet (pp. 155–156). Though the individual sufferer showed jealousy and anger, the Manu'ans believed that a new love would quickly cure a betrayed lover (pp. 105–108). It is possible that Mead failed to understand the shallowness of love in our own society: Romantic love is, "in our civilization, inextricably bound up with ideas of monogamy, exclusiveness, jealousy, and undeviating fidelity" (p. 105). But these are *ideas* and ideology; *behavior* is rather different.

But this complex is rare. Perhaps only the following cultures possess the romantic love value complex: modern urban United States, Northwestern Europe, Polynesia, and the European nobility of the eleventh and twelfth centuries.[21] Certainly, it is to be found in no other major civilization. On the other hand, the *love pattern,* which views love as a basis for the final decision to marry, may be relatively common.

WHY LOVE MUST BE CONTROLLED

Since strong love attachments apparently can occur in any society and since (as we shall show) love is frequently a basis for and prelude to marriage, it must be controlled or channeled in some way. More specifically, the stratification and lineage patterns would be weakened greatly if love's potentially disruptive effects were not kept in check. The importance of this situation may be seen most clearly by considering one of the major functions of the family, status placement, which in every society links the structures of stratification, kinship lines, and mate choice. (To show how the very similar comments which have been made about sex are not quite correct would take us too far afield; in any event, to the extent that they are correct, the succeeding analysis applies equally to the control of sex.)

Both the child's placement in the social structure and choice of mates are socially important because both placement and choice link two kinship lines together. Courtship or mate choice, therefore, cannot be ignored by either family or society. To permit random mating would mean radical change in the existing social structure. If the family as a unit of society is important, then mate choice is too.

Kinfolk or immediate family can disregard the question of who marries whom, only if a marriage is not seen as a link between kin lines, only if no property, power, lineage honor, totemic relationships, and the like are believed to flow from the kin lines through the spouses to their offspring. Universally, however, these are believed to follow kin lines. Mate choice thus has consequences for the social structure. But love may affect mate choice. Both mate choice and love, therefore, are too important to be left to children.

THE CONTROL OF LOVE

Since considerable energy and resources may be required to push youngsters who are in love into proper role behavior, love must be controlled

[21] I am preparing an analysis of this case. The relation of "courtly love" to social structure is complicated.

before it appears. Love relationships must either be kept to a small number or they must be so directed that they do not run counter to the approved kinship linkages. There are only a few institutional patterns by which this control is achieved.

1. Certainly the simplest, and perhaps the most widely used, structural pattern for coping with this problem is child marriage. If the child is betrothed, married, or both before he has had any opportunity to interact intimately as an adolescent with other children, then he has no resources with which to oppose the marriage. He cannot earn a living, he is physically weak, and is socially dominated by his elders. Moreover, strong love attachments occur only rarely before puberty. An example of this pattern was to be found in India, where the young bride went to live with her husband in a marriage which was not physically consummated until much later, within his father's household.[22]

2. Often, child marriage is linked with a second structural pattern, in which the kinship rules define rather closely a class of eligible future spouses. The marriage is determined by birth within narrow limits. Here, the major decision, which is made by elders, is *when* the marriage is to occur. Thus, among the Murngin, *galle,* the father's sister's child, is scheduled to marry *due,* the mother's brother's child.[23] In the case of the "four-class" double-descent system, each individual is a member of *both* a matri-moiety and a patri-moiety and must marry someone who belongs to neither; the four-classes are (1) ego's own class, (2) those whose matri-moiety is the same as ego's but whose patri-moiety is different, (3) those who are in ego's patri-moiety but not in his matri-moiety, and (4) those who are in neither of ego's moieties, that is, who are in the cell diagonally from his own.[24] Problems arise at times under these systems if the appropriate kinship cell—for example, parallel cousin or cross-cousin—is empty.[25] But nowhere, apparently, is the definition so rigid as to exclude some choice and, therefore, some dickering, wrangling, and haggling between the elders of the two families.

[22] Frieda M. Das, *Purdah,* New York: Vanguard, 1932; Kingsley Davis, *The Population of India and Pakistan,* Princeton: Princeton University Press, 1951, p. 112. There was a widespread custom of taking one's bride from a village other than one's own.

[23] W. Lloyd Warner, *Black Civilization,* New York: Harper, 1937, pp. 82–84. They may also become "sweethearts" at puberty; see pp. 86–89.

[24] See Murdock, *op. cit.,* pp. 53 ff. *et passim* for discussions of double-descent.

[25] One adjustment in Australia was for the individuals to leave the tribe for a while, usually eloping, and then to return "reborn" under a different and now appropriate kinship designation. In any event, these marital prescriptions did not prevent love entirely. As Malinowski shows in his early summary of the Australian family systems, although every one of the tribes used the technique of infant betrothal (and close prescription of mate), no tribe was free of elopements, between either the unmarried or the married, and the "motive of sexual love" was always to be found in marriages by elopement. B. Malinowski, *The Family Among the Australian Aborigines,* London: University of London Press, 1913, p. 83.

3. A society can prevent widespread development of adolescent love relationships by socially isolating young people from potential mates, whether eligible or ineligible as spouses. Under such a pattern, elders can arrange the marriages of either children or adolescents with little likelihood that their plans will be disrupted by love attachments. Obviously, this arrangement cannot operate effectively in most primitive societies, where youngsters see one another rather frequently.[26]

Not only is this pattern more common in civilizations than in primitive societies, but is found more frequently in the upper social strata. *Social* segregation is difficult unless it is supported by physical segregation—the harem of Islam, the zenana of India[27]—or by a large household system with individuals whose duty it is to supervise nubile girls. Social segregation is thus expensive. Perhaps the best known example of simple social segregation was found in China, where youthful marriages took place between young people who had not previously met because they lived in different villages; they could not marry fellow-villagers since ideally almost all inhabitants belonged to the same *tsu.*[28]

It should be emphasized that the primary function of physical or social isolation in these cases is to minimize informal or intimate social interaction. Limited social contacts of a highly ritualized or formal type in the presence of elders, as in Japan, have a similar, if less extreme, result.[29]

4. A fourth type of pattern seems to exist, although it is not clear cut; and specific cases shade off toward types three and five. Here, there is close supervision by duennas or close relatives, but not actual social segregation. A high value is placed on female chastity (which perhaps is the case in every major civilization until its "decadence") viewed either as

26 This pattern was apparently achieved in Manus, where on first menstruation the girl was removed from her playmates and kept at "home"—on stilts over a lagoon—under the close supervision of elders. The Manus were prudish, and love occurred rarely or never. Margaret Mead, *Growing Up in New Guinea,* in *From the South Seas,* New York: Morrow, 1939, pp. 163–166, 208.

27 See Das, *op. cit.*

28 For the activities of the *tsu,* see Hsien Chin Hu, *The Common Descent Group in China and Its Functions,* New York: Viking Fund Studies in Anthropology, 10 (1948). For the marriage process, see Marion J. Levy, *The Family Revolution in Modern China,* Cambridge: Harvard University Press, 1949, pp. 87–107. See also Olga Lang, *Chinese Family and Society,* New Haven: Yale University Press, 1946, for comparisons between the old and new systems. In one-half of 62 villages in Ting Hsien Experimental District in Hopei, the largest clan included 50 per cent of the families; in 25 per cent of the villages, the two largest clans held over 90 per cent of the families; I am indebted to Robert M. Marsh who has been carrying out a study of Ching mobility partly under my direction for this reference: F. C. H. Lee, *Ting Hsien. She-hui K'ai-K'uang t'iao-ch'a,* Peiping: Chung-hua p'ing-min Chiao-yu ts'u-chin hui, 1932, p. 54. See also Sidney Gamble, *Ting Hsien: A North China Rural Community,* New York: International Secretariat of the Institute of Pacific Relations, 1954.

29 For Japan, see Shidzué Ishimoto, *Facing Two Ways,* New York: Farrar and Rinehart, 1935, Chapters 6, 8; John F. Embree, *Suye Mura,* Chicago: University of Chicago Press, 1950, Chapters 3, 6.

the product of self-restraint, as among the 17th Century Puritans, or as a marketable commodity. Thus love as play is not developed; marriage is supposed to be considered by the young as a duty and a possible family alliance. This pattern falls between types three and five because love is permitted before marriage, but only between eligibles. Ideally, it occurs only between a betrothed couple, and, except as marital love, there is no encouragement for it to appear at all. Family elders largely make the specific choice of mate, whether or not intermediaries carry out the arrangements. In the preliminary stages youngsters engage in courtship under supervision, with the understanding that this will permit the development of affection prior to marriage.

I do not believe that the empirical data show where this pattern is prevalent, outside of Western Civilization. The West is a special case, because of its peculiar relationship to Christianity, in which from its earliest days in Rome there has been a complex tension between asceticism and love. This type of limited love marked French, English, and Italian upper class family life from the 11th to the 14th Centuries, as well as 17th Century Puritanism in England and New England.[30]

5. The fifth type of pattern permits or actually encourages love relationships, and love is a commonly expected element in mate choice. Choice in this system is *formally* free. In their teens youngsters begin their love play, with or without consummating sexual intercourse, within a group of peers. They may at times choose love partners whom they and others do not consider suitable spouses. Gradually, however, their range of choice is narrowed and eventually their affections center on one individual. This person is likely to be more eligible as a mate according to general social norms, and as judged by peers and parents, than the average individual with whom the youngster formerly indulged in love play.

For reasons that are not yet clear, this pattern is nearly always associated with a strong development of an adolescent peer group system, although the latter may occur without the love pattern. One source of social control, then, is the individual's own teen-age companions, who persistently rate the present and probable future accomplishments of each individual.[31]

[30] I do not mean, of course, to restrict this pattern to these times and places, but I am more certain of these. For the Puritans, see Edmund S. Morgan, *The Puritan Family,* Boston: Public Library, 1944. For the somewhat different practices in New York, see Charles E. Ironside, *The Family in Colonial New York,* New York: Columbia University Press, 1942. See also: A. Abram, *English Life and Manners in the Later Middle Ages,* New York: Dutton, 1913, Chapters 4, 10; Emily J. Putnam, *The Lady,* New York: Sturgis and Walton, 1910, Chapter 4; James Gairdner, editor, *The Paston Letters, 1422–1509,* 4 vols., London: Arber, 1872–1875; Eileen Power, "The Position of Women," in C. G. Crump and E. F. Jacobs, editors, *The Legacy of the Middle Ages,* Oxford: Clarendon, 1926, pp. 414–416.

[31] For those who believe that the young in the United States are totally deluded by love, or believe that love outranks every other consideration, see: Ernest W. Burgess

Another source of control lies with the parents of both boy and girl. In our society, parents threaten, cajole, wheedle, bribe, and persuade their children to "go with the right people," during both the early love play and later courtship phases.[32] Primarily, they seek to control love relationships by influencing the informal social contacts of their children: moving to appropriate neighborhoods and schools, giving parties and helping to make out invitation lists, by making their children aware that certain individuals have ineligibility traits (race, religion, manners, tastes, clothing, and so on). Since youngsters fall in love with those with whom they associate, control over informal relationships also controls substantially the focus of affection. The results of such control are well known and are documented in the more than one hundred studies of homogamy in this country: most marriages take place between couples in the same class, religious, racial, and educational levels.

As Robert Wikman has shown in a generally unfamiliar (in the United States) but superb investigation, this pattern was found among 18th Century Swedish farmer adolescents, was widely distributed in other Germanic areas, and extends in time from the 19th Century back to almost certainly the late Middle Ages.[33] In these cases, sexual intercourse was taken for granted, social contact was closely supervised by the peer group, and final consent to marriage was withheld or granted by the parents who owned the land.

Such cases are not confined to Western society. Polynesia exhibits a similar pattern, with some variation from society to society, the best known examples of which are perhaps Mead's Manu'ans and Firth's Tikopia.[34] Probably the most familiar Melanesian cases are the Trobriands and Dobu,[35] where the systems resemble those of the Kiwai Papuans of the Trans-Fly and the Siuai Papuans of the Solomon Islands.[36] Linton

---

and Paul W. Wallin, *Engagement and Marriage,* New York: Lippincott, 1953, pp. 217–238. Note Karl Robert V. Wikman, *Die Einleitung Der Ehe. Acta Academiae Aboensis (Humaniora)*, 11 (1937), pp. 127 ff. Not only are reputations known because of close association among peers, but songs and poetry are sometimes composed about the girl or boy. Cf., for the Tikopia, Raymond Firth, *We, the Tikopia,* New York: American Book, 1936, pp. 468 ff.; for the Siuai, Douglas L. Oliver, *Solomon Island Society,* Cambridge: Harvard University Press, 1955, pp. 146 ff. The Manu'ans made love in groups of three or four couples; cf. Mead, *Coming of Age in Samoa, op. cit.,* p. 92.

32 Marvin B. Sussman, "Parental Participation in Mate Selection and Its Effect upon Family Continuity," *Social Forces,* 32 (October, 1953), pp. 76–81.

33 Wikman, *op. cit.*

34 Mead, *Coming of Age in Samoa, op. cit.,* pp. 97–108; and Firth, *op. cit.,* pp. 520 ff.

35 Thus Malinowski notes in his "Introduction" to Reo F. Fortune's *The Sorcerers of Dobu,* London: Routledge, 1932, p. xxiii, that the Dobu have similar patterns, the same type of courtship by trial and error, with a gradually tightening union.

36 Gunnar Landtman, *Kiwai Papuans of the Trans-Fly,* London: Macmillan, 1927, pp. 243 ff.; Oliver, *op. cit.,* pp. 153 ff.

found this pattern among the Tanala.[37] Although Radcliffe-Brown holds that the pattern is not common in Africa, it is clearly found among the Nuer, the Kgatla (Tswana-speaking), and the Bavenda (here, without sanctioned sexual intercourse).[38]

A more complete classification, making use of the distinctions suggested in this paper, would show, I believe, that a large minority of known societies exhibit this pattern. I would suggest, moreover, that such a study would reveal that the degree to which love is a usual, expected prelude to marriage is correlated with (1) the degree of free choice of mate permitted in the society and (2) the degree to which husband-wife solidarity is the strategic solidarity of the kinship structure.[39]

LOVE CONTROL AND CLASS

These sociostructural explanations of how love is controlled lead to a subsidiary but important hypothesis: From one society to another, and from one *class* to another within the same society, the sociostructural importance of maintaining kinship lines according to rule will be rated differently by the families within them. Consequently, the degree to which control over mate choice, and therefore over the prevalence of a love pattern among adolescents, will also vary. Since, within any stratified society, this concern with the maintenance of intact and acceptable kin lines will be greater in the upper strata, it follows that noble or upper strata will maintain stricter control over love and courtship behavior than lower strata. The two correlations suggested in the preceding paragraph also apply: husband-wife solidarity is less strategic relative to clan soli-

[37] The pattern apparently existed among the Marquesans as well, but since Linton never published a complete description of this Polynesian society, I omit it here. His fullest analysis, cluttered with secondary interpretations, is in Abram Kardiner, *Psychological Frontiers of Society,* New York: Columbia University Press, 1945. For the Tanala, see Ralph Linton, *The Tanala,* Chicago: Field Museum, 1933, pp. 300–303.

[38] Thus, Radcliffe-Brown: "The African does not think of marriage as a union based on romantic love, although beauty as well as character and health are sought in the choice of a wife," in his "Introduction" to A. R. Radcliffe-Brown and W. C. Daryll Ford, editors, *African Systems of Kinship and Marriage,* London: Oxford University Press, 1950, p. 46. For the Nuer, see E. E. Evans-Pritchard, *Kinship and Marriage Among the Nuer,* Oxford: Clarendon, 1951, pp. 49–58. For the Kgatla, see I. Schapera, *Married Life in an African Tribe,* New York: Sheridan, 1941, pp. 55 ff. For the Bavenda, although the report seems incomplete, see Hugh A. Stayt, *The Bavenda,* London: Oxford University Press, 1931, pp. 111 ff., 145 ff., 154.

[39] The second correlation is developed from Marion J. Levy, *The Family Revolution in China,* Cambridge, Harvard University Press, 1949, p. 179. Levy's formulation ties "romantic love" to that solidarity, and is of little use because there is only one case, the Western culture complex. As he states it, it is almost so by definition.

darity in the upper than in the lower strata, and there is less free choice of mate.

Thus it is that, although in Polynesia generally most youngsters indulged in considerable love play, princesses were supervised strictly.[40] Similarly, in China lower class youngsters often met their spouses before marriage.[41] In our own society, the "upper upper" class maintains much greater control than the lower strata over the informal social contacts of their nubile young. Even among the Dobu, where there are few controls and little stratification, differences in control exist at the extremes: a child betrothal may be arranged between outstanding gardening families, who try to prevent their youngsters from being entangled with wastrel families.[42] In answer to my query about this pattern among the Nuer, Evans-Pritchard writes:

> You are probably right that a wealthy man has more control over his son's affairs than a poor man. A man with several wives has a more authoritarian position in his home. Also, a man with many cattle is in a position to permit or refuse a son to marry, whereas a lad whose father is poor may have to depend on the support of kinsmen. In general, I would say that a Nuer father is not interested in the personal side of things. His son is free to marry any girl he likes and the father does not consider the selection to be his affair until the point is reached when cattle have to be discussed.[43]

The upper strata have much more at stake in the maintenance of the social structure and thus are more strongly motivated to control the courtship and marriage decisions of their young. Correspondingly, their young have much more to lose than lower strata youth, so that upper strata elders *can* wield more power.

[40] E.g., Mead, *Coming of Age in Samoa, op. cit.*, 79, 92, 97–109. Cf. also Firth, *op. cit.*, pp. 520 ff.

[41] Although one must be cautious about China, this inference seems to be allowable from such comments as the following: "But the old men of China did not succeed in eliminating love from the life of the young women. . . . Poor and middle-class families could not afford to keep men and women in separate quarters, and Chinese also met their cousins. . . . Girls . . . sometimes even served customers in their parents' shops." Olga Lang, *op. cit.*, p. 33. According to Fried, farm girls would work in the fields, and farm girls of ten years and older were sent to the market to sell produce. They were also sent to towns and cities as servants. The peasant or pauper woman was not confined to the home and its immediate environs. Morton H. Fried, *Fabric of Chinese Society*, New York: Praeger, 1953, pp. 59–60. Also, Levy (*op. cit.*, p. 111): "Among peasant girls and among servant girls in gentry households some premarital experience was not uncommon, though certainly frowned upon. The methods of preventing such contact were isolation and chaperonage, both of which, in the 'traditional' picture, were more likely to break down in the two cases named than elsewhere."

[42] Fortune, *op. cit.*, p. 30.

[43] Personal letter, dated January 9, 1958. However, the Nuer father can still refuse if he believes the demands of the girl's people are unreasonable. In turn, the girl can cajole her parents to demand less.

CONCLUSION

In this analysis I have attempted to show the integration of love with various types of social structures. As against considerable contemporary opinion among both sociologists and anthropologists, I suggest that love is a universal psychological potential, which is controlled by a range of five structural patterns, all of which are attempts to see to it that youngsters do not make entirely free choices of their future spouses. Only if kin lines are unimportant, and this condition is found in no society as a whole, will entirely free choice be permitted. Some structural arrangements seek to prevent entirely the outbreak of love, while others harness it. Since the kin lines of the upper strata are of greater social importance to them than those of lower strata are to the lower strata members, the former exercise a more effective control over this choice. Even where there is almost a formally free choice of mate—and I have suggested that this pattern is widespread, to be found among a substantial segment of the earth's societies—this choice is guided by peer group and parents toward a mate who will be acceptable to the kin and friend groupings. The theoretical importance of love is thus to be seen in the sociostructural patterns which are developed to keep it from disrupting existing social arrangements.

Passionate Love

Elaine Walster

DEFINITIONS

Liking has been defined by a number of researchers[1] as "a positive attitude toward another, evidenced by a tendency to approach and interact with him." Theorists generally agree on the genesis of liking: individuals like those who reward them.*

Researchers have spent little time defining or investigating *passionate love.* Many theorists simply assume that passionate love is nothing more than very intense liking. We would argue, however, that passionate love is a distinct emotional state. We would argue that a person will experience love only if 1) he is physiologically aroused, and 2) he concludes that love is the appropriate label for his aroused feelings.

PASSIONATE LOVE: A TABOO TOPIC

Most of us would agree that passion is more fascinating than friendship. However, a multitude of researchers have conducted experiments on liking, while very few have explored passionate love.

This report was financed by National Institute of Mental Health Grant MH 16661 and National Science Foundation Grant GS 2932. The theoretical framework I present was developed in collaboration with Dr. Ellen Berscheid, University of Minnesota.

Reprinted from B. I. Murstein (Ed.), *Theories of Attraction and Love,* pp. 85–99.

[1] See e.g. T. M. Newcomb, *The Acquaintance Process.* (New York: Holt, Rinehart, and Winston, 1971); and G. C. Homans, *The Human Group.* (New York: Harcourt, Brace, and World, 1950).

* We use the term *companionate love* to indicate unusually intense *liking* between two persons.

What accounts for this imbalance?

1) First, scientists who wanted to investigate romantic attraction found it very difficult to secure research funds. Granting agencies, sensitive to the feelings of legislators and the public, were nervous about even considering proposals whose titles contained the offensive words "Love" or "Sex." Even today, whenever a researcher is ill-mannered enough to affix such a title to his proposal, alert bureaucrats quickly expurgate the offensive term and substitute the euphemism, "social affiliation."

2) Psychologists did not themselves acknowledge the legitimacy of investigating passionate love. They often ridiculed colleagues who began conducting experiments on this taboo topic. To study love was to be "soft-headed," "unscientific," or to possess a flair for the trivial. It is interesting to note that early in their careers some of our most eminent social psychologists conducted one—and only one—study on romantic attraction. Professional reaction to their research uniformly led them to decide to investigate other topics.

3) Psychologists tend to assume that in the laboratory one can only study mild and quickly developing phenomena. Although poets argue that love may occur "at first sight," psychologists have had less confidence that one can generate passionate love in a two-hour laboratory experiment. Thus, many researchers erroneously assumed that passionate love could only be studied in the field.

Suddenly, the situation changed. The humanists invaded psychology, and the study of tender emotions became respectable. Masters and Johnson's[2] impressive research demonstrated that even sex could be examined in the laboratory. (Ironically, these pioneers were attacked by the public for failing to investigate love as well as sex.) In the last five years more psychologists have begun to study romantic love than investigated the phenomenon in the history of psychology.

The problem now is not finding respectability but finding out some facts. Presently, when faced with requests for information about love and sex, chagrined psychologists must admit that "they really don't know love at all." Hopefully, in this conference we can gain a better understanding about this vital—and entertaining—topic. In this paper, I will propose a theoretical framework which may give us a better understanding of passionate love.

"WHAT IS THIS THING CALLED LOVE?"

Interpersonal attraction and companionate love seem like sensible phenomena. One can predict quite well how much a person will like another,

[2] W. H. Masters and V. E. Johnson, *Human Sexual Response.* (Boston: Little, Brown, and Company, 1966).

if he knows to what extent the other rewards or punishes the person. Reward has so predictable an impact on liking that Byrne *et al* [3] could with confidence propose an exact correspondence between reinforcement and liking: ("Attraction towards X is a positive linear function of the proportion of positive reinforcements received from X or expected from X.") Data support their formulation.

Sometimes passionate love seems to operate in a sensible fashion. Some practical people have been known to fall in love with those beautiful, wise, entertaining, and kind people who offer affection or material rewards to them. Generally, however, passionate love does not seem to fit so neatly into the reinforcement paradigm. Individuals do *not* always feel passionate about the person who provides the most rewards with the greatest consistency. Passion sometimes develops under conditions that would seem more likely to provoke aggression and hatred than love. For example, reinforcement theorists argue that "we like those who like us and reject those who dislike us." Yet individuals experience intense love for those who have rejected them.

A woman discovers her husband is seeing another. The pain and suffering the jealous wife experiences at this discovery cause her to realize how much she loves her husband.

Lovers pine away for the girls who spurn their affection. For example, a recent Associated Press release reports the desperate excuse of an Italian lover who kidnapped his former sweetheart: "'The fact that she rejected me only made me want and love her more,' he tearfully explained."

Reinforcement theorists tell us that "frustration always breeds aggression." Yet, inhibited sexuality is assumed to be the foundation of romantic feelings. Freud even argued that:

Some obstacle is necessary to swell the tide of libido to its height; and at all periods of history whenever natural barriers in the way of satisfaction have not sufficed, mankind has erected conventional ones in order to enjoy love.[4]

The observation that passionate love flourishes in settings which would seem to thwart its development has always been puzzling to social scientists. Poets attribute such inexplicable phenomena to the essential illogic of love. Scientists, who refuse to acknowledge that anything is inexplicable, do not have such an easy way out.

Happily, we believe that a theoretical framework exists which makes the "illogical" phenomena of passionate love explicable and predictable.

[3] D. Byrne, O. London, and K. Reeves, "The effect of physical attractiveness, sex, and attitude similarity on interpersonal attraction," *Journal of Personality*, 1968, *36*, 259–271.

[4] S. Freud, "The most prevalent form of degradation in erotic life," in E. Jones (ed.), *Collected Papers, 4*. (London: Hogarth, 1925), pp. 203–216.

SCHACHTER'S TWO-COMPONENT THEORY

On the basis of an ingenious series of experiments, Schachter[5] proposed a paradigm for understanding human emotional response. He argues that in order for a person to experience true emotion, two factors must coexist: 1) The individual must be physiologically aroused, and 2) It must be reasonable to interpret his stirred-up state in emotional terms. Schachter argued that neither physiological arousal nor appropriate cognitions *alone* is sufficient to produce an emotional experience.

It is possible to manipulate an individual's physiological arousal artificially. A drug, adrenalin, exists whose effects mimic the discharge of the sympathetic nervous system. Shortly after one receives an injection of adrenalin, systolic blood pressure increases markedly, heart rate increases somewhat, cutaneous blood flow decreases, muscle and cerebral blood flow increase, blood sugar and lactic acid concentration increase, and respiration rate increases slightly. The individual who has been injected with adrenalin experiences palpitation, tremor, and sometimes flushing and accelerated breathing. These reactions are identical to the physiological reactions which accompany a variety of natural emotional states.

An injection of adrenalin will not, by itself, however, engender an emotional response in a person. When an individual is injected with adrenalin and asked to introspect, he will report either no emotional response or, at best, report feeling "as if" he might be experiencing some emotion.[6] Individuals make statements such as "I feel *as if* I were afraid." The person who has been injected with adrenalin perceives that something is not quite authentic about his reactions. Something is missing.

Schachter argues that what is missing is an appropriate label for the physiological reactions one is experiencing. If one could lead the drugged individual to attribute his stirred-up state to some emotion-arousing event (rather than attributing it to the injection of adrenalin which he received), Schachter argues that he would experience a "true" emotion.

The researcher who wishes to test the notion that physiological arousal and appropriate cognitions are separate and indispensable components of a true emotional experience, is faced with the challenging task of separately manipulating these two components. In a classic study, Schachter and Singer[7] conceived of a way to do just that. Volunteers were recruited

[5] S. Schachter, "The interaction of cognitive and physiological determinants of emotional state," in L. Berkowitz (ed.), *Advances in Experimental Social Psychology, 1.* (New York: Academic Press, 1964), pp. 49–80.

[6] G. Marañon, "Contribution a l'etude de l'action emotive de l'adrenaline," *Revue Francaise Endocrinalogia,* 1924, *2,* 301–325.

[7] S. Schachter and J. Singer, "Cognitive, social, and physiological determinants of emotional state," *Psychological Review,* 1962, *69,* 379–399.

for an experiment which the experimenters claimed was designed to investigate the effects of a new vitamin compound, Suproxin, on vision.

Manipulating Physiological Arousal: Volunteers were injected with a substance which was identified as Suproxin. Actually, one half of the students were injected with epinephrine (½ cc of a 1:1000 solution of Winthrop Laboratory's Suprarenin). Such an injection causes the intense physiological reactions described earlier. One half received a placebo (½ cc of saline solution).

Manipulating an Appropriate Explanation: Schachter wished to lead some of the volunteers to correctly attribute their physiological state to a nonemotional cause (the injection). He wished to lead others to attribute their stirred-up state to an emotional cause.

Thus, in one condition (the *Non-Emotional Attribution* condition), individuals were given a complete explanation of how the shot would affect them. They were warned that in 15 to 20 minutes the injection of "Suproxin" would cause palpitation, tremor, etc. Presumably, when students began to experience these symptoms, they could properly attribute their stirred-up state to the shot and would *not* attribute their excitement to the activities in which they were engaging at the time the adrenalin began to take effect.

In the *Emotional Attribution* conditions, things were arranged to *discharge* students from attributing their stirred-up state to the shot. One group of volunteers was given no information about possible side effects of the shot. A second group of volunteers was deliberately misled as to the potential side effects of the shot. It was assumed that volunteers who received either no information or incorrect information would be unlikely to attribute their tremors and palpitations to the shot. After all, these symptoms took 20 minutes to develop. Instead, the authors hoped that volunteers would attribute their arousal to whatever they happened to be doing when the drug took effect. The authors then arranged things so that what volunteers "happened to be doing" was participating in either a gay, happy, social interaction or participating in a tense, explosive interaction.

If the subject had been assigned to the *Euphoria* condition, his fellow student (who was actually a confederate) had been trained to generate excitement while they waited 20 minutes for the experiment to begin. As soon as the experimenter left the room, the confederate began "acting up." He shot paper wads into the wastebasket, built a paper tower which he sent crashing to the floor and generally kidded around.

In the *Anger* setting, the confederate had been trained to make the subject angry. The confederate first complained about the experimental procedures. He became especially indignant on encountering the questionnaire they had been asked to fill out (and which admittedly asked stupid and offensive questions). Finally, the confederate slammed his questionnaire to the floor and stomped out.

The authors assessed subjects' emotional reactions to the confederate's behavior in two ways. Observers stationed behind a one-way mirror assessed to what extent the subject caught the stooge's euphoric or angry mood; secondly, subjects were asked to describe their moods and to estimate how euphoric and angry they felt.

Schachter and Singer predicted that those subjects who had received an adrenalin injection would have stronger emotional reactions than would subjects who had received a placebo or had received an adrenalin injection but had been warned of exactly what physiological changes they should expect. The data supported these hypotheses. The experiment thus supported the contention that both physiological arousal and appropriate cognitions are indispensable components of a true emotional experience. Schachter and Wheeler[8] provide additional support for this contention.

THE TWO-COMPONENT THEORY AND PASSIONATE LOVE

The discovery that almost any sort of intense physiological arousal—if properly interpreted—will precipitate an emotional experience has intriguing implications. We were particularly intrigued by the possibility that Schachter's "two-component" theory might help explain a heretofore inexplicable phenomena—passionate love.

As long as researchers were busily absorbed in figuring out how passionate love could be integrated into the reinforcement paradigm, we made little progress. The observation that negative experiences often lead to increased evaluation remained inexplicable.

A sudden insight solved our dilemma. Two components are necessary for a passionate experience: arousal and appropriate cognitions. Perhaps negative experiences do not increase love by somehow improving one's evaluation of the other (beneficially altering his cognitions). Perhaps negative experiences are effective in inducing love because they intensify the second component—arousal.

We would suggest that perhaps it does not really matter how one produces an agitated state in an individual. Stimuli that usually produce sexual arousal, gratitude, anxiety, guilt, loneliness, hatred, jealousy, or confusion may all increase one's physiological arousal, and thus increase the intensity of his emotional experience. As long as one attributes his agitated state to passion, he should experience true passionate love. As soon as he ceases to attribute his tumultuous feelings to passion, love should die.

[8] S. Schachter and L. Wheeler, "Epinephrine, chlorpromazine, and amusement," *Journal of Abnormal Social Psychology,* 1962, *65,* 121–128.

Does any evidence exist to support our contention? Some early observers noticed that any form of strong emotional arousal breeds love (although not, of course, interpreting this relationship in Schachterian terms). Finck, an early psychologist, concluded:

> Love can only be excited by strong and vivid emotion, and it is almost immaterial whether these emotions are agreeable or disagreeable. The Cid wooed the proud heart of Diana Ximene, whose father he had slain, by shooting one after another of her pet pigeons. Such persons as arouse in us only weak emotions or none at all, are obviously least likely to incline us toward them. . . . Our aversion is most likely to be bestowed on individuals who, as the phrase goes, are neither 'warm' nor 'cold'; whereas impulsive, choleric people, though they may readily offend us, are just as capable of making us warmly attached to them.[9]

Unfortunately, experimental evidence does not yet exist to support the contention that almost any form of high arousal, if properly labeled, will deepen passion. There are, however, a few studies designed to test other hypotheses, which provide some minimal support for our contention.*

Since it was the juxtaposition of misery and ecstasy in romantic love that we initially found so perplexing, let us first examine the relation between negative experiences and love.

UNPLEASANT EMOTIONAL STATES: FACILITATORS OF PASSION?

That negative reinforcements produce strong emotional reactions in all animals is not in doubt. There is some evidence that under the right conditions such unpleasant, but arousing, states as fear, rejection, and frustration do enhance romantic passion.

Frightening a person is a very good way of producing intense psychological arousal for a substantial period of time.[10]

An intriguing study by Brehm *et al*[11] demonstrates that a frightened man is a romantic man. Brehm *et al* tested the hypothesis that "a person's attraction to another would be multiplied by prior arousal from an irrele-

* These studies are only "minimally supportive" because the authors investigate only liking, not passionate loving—a phenomenon we have argued is unique. Whether or not the same results would occur in a romantic context must yet be determined.

[9] H. T. Finck, *Romantic Love and Personal Beauty: Their Development, Causal Relations, Historic and National Peculiarities.* (London: Macmillan, 1891), p. 240.

[10] See A. F. Ax. "Fear and anger in humans," *Psychosomatic Medicine,* 1953, *15,* 433–442, S. Wolf and H. G. Wolff, *Human Gastric Function* (2nd edition). (London: Oxford University Press, 1947); and J. Schachter, "Pain, fear, and anger in hypertensives and normotensives: a psycho-physiological Study," *Psychosomatic Medicine,* 1957, *19,* 17–24.

[11] J. W. Brehm, M. Gatz, G. Goethals, J. McCrimmon, and L. Ward, "Physiological arousal and interpersonal attraction," Mimeo, 1970.

vant event." In this experiment, some men were led to believe that they would soon receive three "pretty stiff" electrical shocks. Half of the men, "Threat" subjects, were allowed to retain this erroneous expectation throughout the experiment. Half of the men, "Threat-Relief," were frightened and then, sometime later, were told that the experimenter had made an error; they had been assigned to the control group and would receive no shock. The remainder of the men were assigned to a control group, in which the possibility of their receiving shock was not even mentioned.

Men were then introduced to a young co-ed, and asked how much they liked her.

The Threat subjects who expected to be shocked in the future should be quite frightened at the time they meet the girl. The Threat-Relief subjects who had just learned they would not be shocked should be experiencing vast relief when they meet the girl. Both the frightened and the frightened-relieved men should be more aroused than are men in the control group. Brehm predicted, as we would, that Threat and Threat-Relief subjects would like the girl more than would control subjects. Brehm's expectations were confirmed; threatened men experienced more liking for the girl (and did not differ in their liking) than did control group men, who had never been frightened. An irrelevant frightening event, then, does seem to facilitate attraction.

REJECTION: AN ANTECEDENT OF PASSION

Rejection is always disturbing. And generally when a person is rejected he has a strong emotional reaction. Usually he experiences embarrassment, pain, or anger. Although it is probably most reasonable for a rejected person to label his agitation in this way, if our hypothesis is correct, it should be possible, under the right conditions, to induce a rejected individual to label his emotional response as "love" as well as "hate."

Some slight evidence that passionate love *or* hate may emerge from rejection comes from several laboratory experiments designed to test other hypotheses.[12]

Let us consider one of these experiments and the way a Schachterian might reinterpret these data.

The experiment of Jacobs *et al* was designed to determine how changes in the self-esteem of college students affected their receptivity to love and affection. First, students took a number of personality tests (the *MMPI,*

[12] J. E. Dittes, "Attractiveness of group as function of self-esteem and acceptance by group," *Journal of Abnormal and Social Psychology,* 1959, *59,* 77–82; E. Walster, "The effect of self-esteem on romantic liking," *Journal of Experimental Social Psychology,* 1965, *1,* 184–197; and L. Jacobs, E. Walster, and E. Berscheid, "Self-esteem and attraction," *Journal of Personality and Social Psychology,* 1971, *17,* 84–91.

Rorschach, etc.) A few weeks later, a psychologist returned an analysis of his personality to each student. Half of the students were given a flattering personality report. The reports stressed their sensitivity, honesty, originality, and freedom of outlook. (Undoubtedly this flattering personality report confirmed many of the wonderful things the students already thought about themselves.) Half of the students received an insulting personality report. The report stressed their immaturity, weak personality, conventionality, and lack of leadership ability. This critical report was naturally most upsetting for students.

Soon after receiving their analyses, the males got acquainted individually with a young female college student (actually, this girl was an experimental confederate). Half of the time the girl treated the boy in a warm, affectionate, and accepting way. Under such conditions, the men who had received the critical personality evaluation were far more attracted to her than were their more confident counterparts. (Presumably, the previous irrelevant arousal engendered by rejection facilitated the subsequent development of affection.)

Half of the time the girl was cold and rejecting. Under these conditions, a dramatic reversal occurred; the previously rejected men disliked the girl more than did their more confident counterparts. (Presumably, under these conditions, the low self-esteem individual's agitation was transformed to hatred.)

An irrelevant, painful event, then, can incite various strong emotional reactions toward others. Depending on how he labels his feelings, the individual may experience either intensive attraction or intense hostility.

FRUSTRATION AND CHALLENGE: FACILITATORS OF PASSION

Socrates, Ovid, Terence, the Kama Sutra and "Dear Abby" are all in agreement about one thing: the person whose affection is easily won will inspire less passion than the person whose affection is hard to win.

Vassilikos poetically elucidated the principle that frustration fuels passion while continual gratification dims it:

> Once upon a time there was a little fish who was a bird from the waist up and who was madly in love with a little bird who was a fish from the waist up. So the Fish-Bird kept saying to the Bird-Fish: "Oh, why were we created so that we can never live together? You in the wind and I in the wave. What a pity for both of us." And the Bird-Fish would answer: "No, what luck for both of us. This way we'll always be in love because we'll always be separated." [13]

Some provisional evidence that the hard-to-get person may engender unusual passion in the eventually successful suitor comes from Aronson

[13] V. Vassilikos, *The Plant; the Well; the Angel: A Trilogy*. Translated from the Greek by Edmund and Mary Keeley (1st American ed.). (New York: Knopf, 1964), p. 131.

and Linder.[14] These authors tested the hypothesis that: "A gain in esteem is a more potent reward than invariant esteem." They predicted that a person would be better liked if his positive regard was difficult to acquire than if it was easily had.

This hypothesis was tested in the following way: Subjects were required to converse with a confederate (who appeared to be another naive subject) over a series of seven meetings. After each meeting, the subject discovered (secretly) how her conversation partner felt about her. How the confederate "felt" was systematically varied. In one condition the girl expressed a negative impression of the subject after their first meetings. (She described the subject as being a dull conversationalist, a rather ordinary person, not very intelligent, as probably not having many friends, etc.). Only after the partners had become well acquainted did she begin expressing favorable opinions of the subject. In another condition, from the first, the confederate expressed only positive opinions about the subject.

As Aronson and Linder predicted, subjects liked the confederate whose affection was hard to win better than they liked the confederate whose high opinion was readily obtained.

The preceding evidence is consistent with our suggestion that under the right conditions, a hard-to-get girl should generate more passion than the constantly rewarding girl. The aloof girl's challenge may excite the suitor; her momentary rejection may shake his self-esteem. In both cases, such arousal may intensify the suitor's feelings toward her.

The preceding analysis lends some credence to the argument that the juxtaposition of agony and ecstasy in passionate love is not entirely accidental. (The original meaning of "passion" was, in fact, "agony"—for example, as in Christ's passion.) Loneliness, deprivation, frustration, hatred, and insecurity may in fact supplement a person's romantic experiences. Passion requires physiological arousal, and all of the preceding states are certainly arousing.

PLEASANT EMOTIONAL STATES: FACILITATORS OF PASSION?

We would like to make it clear that, theoretically, passion need not include a negative component. The positive reinforcements of discovery, excitement, companionship, and playful-joy can generate as intense an arousal as that stirred by fear, frustration, or rejection. For example, in many autobiographical accounts, entirely joyful (albeit brief) passionate encounters are described.[15]

[14] E. Aronson and D. Linder, "Gain and loss of esteem as determinants of interpersonal attractiveness," *Journal of Experimental Social Psychology*, 1965, *1*, 156–171.

[15] For example, I. Duncan, *Isadora*. (New York: Award Books, 1968).

SEXUAL GRATIFICATION: A FACILITATOR OF PASSION

Sexual experiences can be enormously rewarding and enormously arousing. Masters and Johnson point out that sexual intercourse induces hyperventilation, tachycardia, and marked increases in blood pressure.[16] And, religious advisors, school counselors, and psychoanalysts to the contrary—sexual gratification has undoubtedly generated as much passionate love as has sexual continence.

Valins[17] demonstrated that even the erroneous belief that another has excited one (sexually or aesthetically) will facilitate attraction. Valins recruited male college students for a study of males' physiological reactions to sexual stimuli. The sexual stimuli he utilized were ten semi-nude *Playboy* photographs. The subjects were told that while they scrutinized these photographs, their heart rate would be amplified and recorded. They were led to believe that their heart rates altered markedly to some of the slides but that they had no reaction at all to others. (Valins assumed that the subjects would interpret an alteration in heart rate as sexual enthusiasm.)

The subjects' liking for the "arousing" and "nonarousing" slides was then assessed in three ways. Regardless of the measure used, the men markedly preferred the pin-ups they thought had aroused them to those that had not affected their heart rate. 1) They were asked to rate how "attractive or appealing" each pin-up was. They preferred the pin-ups they believed were arousing to all others. 2) They were offered a pin-up in remuneration for participating in the experiment. They chose the arousing pin-ups more often than the nonarousing ones. 3) Finally, they were interviewed a month later (in a totally different context) and they still markedly preferred the arousing pin-ups to the others.

NEED SATISFACTION: A FACILITATOR OF PASSION

Although psychologists tend to focus almost exclusively on the contribution of sex to love, other rewards can have an equally important emotional impact. People have a wide variety of needs, and at any stage of life many of one's needs must remain unsatisfied. When any important unsatisfied need is recognized or met, the emotional response which accompanies such reinforcement could provide fuel for passion. To the adolescent boy who has been humored, coddled, and babied at home, the girl who finally recognizes his masculinity may be an over-powering joy. The good, steady, reliable, hard-working father may be captivated when

16 Masters and Johnson, *op. cit.*

17 S. Valins, "Cognitive effects of false heart-rate feedback," *Journal of Personality and Social Psychology,* 1966, *4,* 400–408.

an alert lady recognizes that he has the potential to be a playful and reckless lover.

To the person who has been deprived of such rewards, an intelligent, artistic, witty, beautiful, athletic, or playful companion may prove a passionate and absorbing joy.

LABELING

We are proposing a two-factor theory of passionate love. Yet the preceding discussion has focused almost exclusively on one factor. We have concentrated on demonstrating that physiological arousal is a crucial component of passionate love, and that fear, pain, and frustration as well as discovery and delight may contribute to the passionate experience.

We should now at least remind the reader that according to our theory an individual will be incapable of experiencing "love" unless he's prepared to define his feelings in that way.

CULTURAL ENCOURAGEMENT OF LOVE

In our culture, it is expected that everyone will eventually fall in love. Individuals are strongly encouraged to interpret a wide range of confused feelings as love. Linton makes this point in a somewhat harsh observation:

> All societies recognize that there are occasional violent emotional attachments between persons of the opposite sex, but our present American culture is practically the only one which has attempted to capitalize on these and make them the basis for marriage. The hero of the modern American movie is always a romantic lover, just as the hero of an old Arab epic is always an epileptic. A cynic may suspect that in any ordinary population the percentage of individuals with capacity for romantic love of the Hollywood type was about as large as that of persons able to throw genuine epileptic fits.[18]

Individuals are often encouraged to interpret certain confused or mixed feelings as love, because our culture insists that certain reactions are acceptable if one is madly in love. For example, the delightful experience of sexual intercourse can be frankly labeled as "sexual fun" by a man. Such an interpretation of what she is experiencing is probably less acceptable to his partner. She (and her parents) are undoubtedly happier if she attributes her abandoned behavior to love.

Margaret Mead interprets jealousy in one way:

> Jealousy is not a barometer by which the depth of love may be read. It merely records the degree of the lover's insecurity. It is a negative, miserable state of feeling, having its origin in a sense of insecurity and inferiority.[19]

[18] R. Linton, *The Study of Man*. (New York: Appleton-Century, 1936), p. 175.
[19] M. Mead, in A. M. Krich, *The Anatomy of Love*. (New York: Dell, 1960).

Jealous people, however, usually interpret their jealous reactions in quite another way; jealous feelings are taken as evidence of passionate love rather than inferiority. Thus, in this culture, a jealous man is a loving man rather than an embarrassed man.

Thus, whether or not an individual is susceptible to "falling in love" should depend on the expectations of his culture and his reference groups.

INDIVIDUAL EXPECTATIONS

An individual's own expectations should also determine how likely he is to experience love.

The individual who thinks of himself as a nonromantic person should fall in love less often than should an individual who assumes that love is inevitable. The nonromantic may experience the same feelings that the romantic does, but he will code them differently.

Similarly, individuals who feel they are unlovable should have a difficult time finding love. Individuals convey their expectations in very subtle ways to others, and these expectations influence the way one's partner labels *his* reactions. The insecure girl who complains to her boyfriend: "You don't love me, you just think you do. If you loved me you wouldn't treat me this way," and then itemizes evidence of his neglect, may, by automatically interpreting her boyfriend's actions in a damaging way, effect an alteration in his feelings for her. Alternately, a girl with a great deal of self-confidence, may (by her unconscious guidance) induce a normally unreceptive gentleman to label his feelings for her as love.

Liking and Loving

Zick Rubin

LOVE, what is it? Answ. 'Tis very much like light,
a thing that everybody knows, and yet
none can tell what to make of it.

—LADIES DICTIONARY (1694)

Setting out to devise measures of love is like setting out to prepare a gourmet dish with a thousand different recipes but no pots and pans. The recipes for love abound. Throughout history poets, essayists, novelists, philosophers, theologians, psychologists, sociologists, and other men and women of goodwill have written more about love than about virtually any other topic. The index to my edition of Bartlett's *Familiar Quotations* lists 769 references to "love," second only to "man" with 843. But whereas the nature of love has long been a prime topic of discourse and debate, the number of behavioral scientists who have conducted empirical research on love can be counted on one's fingers. And, until recently, the tools with which such research might have been conducted have not existed.

The state of our knowledge about interpersonal attraction has advanced considerably in the past two decades, but primarily through research on liking rather than research directly concerned with love. And while liking and loving are surely close relatives, they are by no means identical. The bridge between research on liking and the extensive writings on love remains to be built.

Here I will report on my own initial endeavor to help build this bridge. My goal was to develop and validate a self-report measure of romantic

---

Abridged from Zick Rubin, *Liking and Loving: An Invitation to Social Psychology*, New York: Holt, Rinehart and Winston, 1973, pp. 211–225, with permission of the author and the publisher.

love. By the adjective "romantic," I do not wish to connote all the trappings of the romantic ideal of the Middle Ages. I use the word simply to distinguish the sort of love that may exist between unmarried, opposite-sex partners from such other related forms as love between children and their parents, close friends, and men and God. The fact that the same word, *love,* may be applied to all of these sorts of relationships must be more than linguistic accident. There are undoubtedly important common elements among these overtly different manifestations. As a starting point for my research, however, it seemed wiser to restrict my attention to a single context.

EROS AND AGAPE

To anchor my attempt to measure love at one end with the work of the "liking researchers," I decided from the start to conceptualize love as an attitude that a person holds toward a particular other person. As such, love—like liking—is an invisible package of feelings, thoughts, and behavioral predispositions within an individual. But I also assumed that the content of this attitude is not the same as that of liking, even extremely strong liking. To determine the content of the attitude to be called love I would have to look elsewhere, to the many prescriptions provided through history.

"How do I love thee? Let me count the ways," declared Elizabeth Barrett Browning, thereby alluding to the most basic form of measurement. My first problem was to decide which ways to count. What Shakespeare defined as "a spirit all compact of fire" has been defined by others in such diverse ways as a "centrifugal act of the soul" (Ortega y Gassett), "a sickness full of woes" (Samuel Daniel), and "not ever having to say you're sorry" (Erich Segal). For Freud, love is a push from within, produced by the sublimation of overtly sexual impulses. For Plato it is a pull from ahead, engendered by the search for the ultimate good. "There are so many sorts of love," Voltaire wrote, "that one does not know where to seek a definition of it." In the midst of all of these conceptions and varieties, however, one dimension stands out as central. This is the opposition of love as *needing* and love as *giving.*

The equation of love with a physical or emotional need can be traced back at least as far as Sappho's symptomatology of love-sickness, offered in the sixth century B.C. The defining features of love, in terms of this conception, are powerful desires to be in the other's presence, to make physical contact, to be approved of, to be cared for. In its most extreme form the love-need appears as a passionate desire to possess and to be fulfilled by another person, corresponding to what the Greeks called *eros.* In more contemporary psychological terms, we can identify the need conception of love with *attachment,* as exemplified by the bonds formed between infants and their parents.

In apparent contrast to the conception of love as a cluster of needs is the conception of love as giving to another person. This is the aspect of love emphasized in the New Testament, epitomized by St. John's declaration, "God is love." Contemporary psychological definitions also depict the lover as the ultimate altruist. For Erich Fromm, "Love is the active concern for the life and growth of that which we love." [1] According to Harry Stack Sullivan, "When the satisfaction or the security of another person becomes as significant to one as is one's own satisfaction or security, then the state of love exists." [2] Love as giving corresponds to what the Greeks called *agape* and to what I will call *caring.*

It can be argued that attachment is a less mature form of love than caring. Whereas infants develop strong attachments toward their parents, for example, caring is a phenomenon that typically does not appear until somewhat later in life. (In Sullivan's view, people first learn to care about others in the context of childhood friendships.) Abraham Maslow associates attachment with people's "deficiency needs" for acceptance and approval. He suggests that "love hunger is a deficiency disease exactly as is salt hunger or the avitaminoses," and, as such, is an immature form of love. People who have reached a higher state of "self-actualization," in Maslow's framework, have already satisfied their deficiency need for love. D-love ("D" for "Deficiency") is replaced by B-love ("B" for "Being"), which is less needful and dependent, and more autonomous and giving.[3]

Maslow's analysis of love implies that attachment and caring stand opposed to one another, and that the more there is of one the less there will be of the other. But it is doubtful that such an opposition corresponds to the actual nature of love relationships. It seems more likely that as a couple's relationship becomes increasingly close, it will be associated with both increased attachment and increased caring. Clinical psychologist David Orlinsky suggests, for example, that attachment and caring merge to form a "dual feeling-impulse," which may be equated with love.[4]

Rather than equate love with attachment or with caring, therefore, I would consider both to be basic components of love. Both attachment and caring remain essentially *individual* conceptions, however, referring

[1] Erich Fromm, *The Art of Loving,* Bantam ed. (New York: Harper & Row, 1956), p. 22.

[2] Harry Stack Sullivan, *Conceptions of Modern Psychiatry,* 2d ed. (New York: Norton, 1953), pp. 42–43.

[3] Abraham H. Maslow, "Deficiency Motivation and Growth Motivation," in Marshall R. Jones (Ed.), *Nebraska Symposium on Motivation, 1955* (Lincoln: University of Nebraska Press, 1955).

[4] David Orlinsky, "Love Relationships in the Life Cycle: A Developmental Interpersonal Perspective," in Herbert A. Otto (Ed.), *Love Today: A New Exploration* (New York: Association Press, 1972).

to inclinations within one person's mind or heart. But there is also an aspect of love that can only be attributed to the relationship between two people, rather than to the two parties individually. Martin Buber makes this point when he talks about the "I–Thou" relationship:

> Love does not cling to an I, as if the Thou were merely its "content" or object; it is *between* I and Thou. Whoever does not know this . . . does not know love, even if he should ascribe to it the feelings that he lives through, experiences, enjoys, and expresses.[5]

It seems useful, therefore, to postulate a third component of love, which refers to the bond or link between two people. This component may be manifest most clearly by close and confidential communication between two people, through nonverbal as well as verbal channels. I will call this third component *intimacy*.

Before constructing a measure of love, it was important to have an idea of how it might be distinguished from liking. In most of the existing research the evaluative component of liking is typically given greatest emphasis. A "likable" person is someone who is viewed as good or desirable on a number of dimensions. In our predominantly "task-oriented" society, the critical dimensions often seem to be task-related ones. We like people who are intelligent, competent, and trustworthy—the sorts of people whom we are disposed to work with or to vote for (as in "I Like Ike").

What would we expect to be the empirical relationships between one person's love and his liking for another person? One would certainly expect at least a moderately positive evaluation of another person to be a prerequisite for the establishment of attachment, caring, and intimacy. Thus, it would be surprising if liking and loving were not at least moderately correlated with one another. But whereas liking and loving may have much in common, we would hesitate to equate the two phenomena. People often express liking for a person whom they would not claim to love in the least. In other instances they may declare their love for someone whom they cannot reasonably be said to like very well.

A starting assumption in my attempt to develop self-report scales of liking and loving, therefore, was that they should represent moderately correlated, but nevertheless distinct, dimensions of one person's attitude toward another person. My study consisted of three stages. First, I constructed parallel self-report scales of liking and loving that met the requirements of the starting assumption. Second, I examined the ways in which the scores of members of dating couples on each of the two scales related to a variety of other things about them, including their plans for marriage. Third, I proceeded to assess the usefulness of the love scale in

[5] Martin Buber, *I and Thou* (New York: Scribner's, 1970), p. 66.

predicting people's subsequent behavior and the course of their relationships. I will describe each of these steps in the following sections.[6]

PUTTING LOVE ON A SCALE

The first step in scale construction was to make up seventy statements reflecting aspects of one person's attitudes toward a particular other person. The items spanned a wide range of thoughts, feelings, and behavioral predispositions—for example, "How much fun is ________ to be with?" "How much do you trust ________?" "To what extent are you physically attracted to ________?" "How much does ________ get on your nerves?" As a check upon my own initial intuitions, I asked a number of friends and acquaintances of both sexes to sort the items into "liking" and "loving" sets, based on their own understandings of the meaning of the two terms. After making revisions suggested by these raters' judgments. I asked 198 undergraduates at the University of Michigan to indicate how much they agreed with each statement in terms of their feelings toward their boyfriend or girlfriend (if they had one), and again in terms of their feelings toward a "platonic friend" of the opposite sex. I then subjected these ratings to a statistical technique called factor analysis, which serves to indicate which sets of items form internally consistent clusters. This procedure led to the specification of two nine-item scales,* one of love and the other of liking (see Table 1).

On the whole, the content of the two scales corresponds closely to the conceptions of liking and loving outlined in the previous section. The love scale includes items that seem to tap the postulated components of attachment (e.g., "If I were lonely, my first thought would be to seek ________ out"); caring (e.g., "One of my primary concerns is ________'s welfare"); and intimacy (e.g., "I feel that I can confide in ________ about virtually everything"). The items on the liking scale focus on the favorable evaluation of the other person on such dimensions as adjustment, maturity, and good judgment. The close fit between the scales and the preceding conceptual discussion is not accidental. Rather, my own working definitions of liking and loving were to a large extent given focus by the results of the scale-development procedure.

I now had two paper-and-pencil scales with a reasonable degree of what psychological testers call "face validity"; that is, the content of each scale approximated people's understandings of what liking and loving

[6] My approach toward conceptualizing and measuring love followed the general strategy outlined by Lee J. Cronbach and Paul E. Meehl in "Construct Validity in Psychological Tests," *Psychological Bulletin,* 1955, *52,* 281–302.

* The original love and liking scales each contained thirteen items. They were later condensed to the current nine-item versions.

should mean. Such face validity did not necessarily imply that the scales would be of any use, however. If, for example, people tended to respond to the items in ways they thought would "look good," rather than in terms of their real feelings, then the scales might measure social anxiety

TABLE 1
LOVE-SCALE AND LIKING-SCALE ITEMS

Love Scale

1. I feel that I can confide in ——— about virtually everything.
2. I would do almost anything for ———.
3. If I could never be with ———, I would feel miserable.
4. If I were lonely, my first thought would be to seek ——— out.
5. One of my primary concerns is ———'s welfare.
6. I would forgive ——— for practically anything.
7. I feel responsible for ———'s well-being.
8. I would greatly enjoy being confided in by ———.
9. It would be hard for me to get along without ———.

Liking Scale

1. I think that ——— is unusually well-adjusted.
2. I would highly recommend ——— for a responsible job.
3. In my opinion, ——— is an exceptionally mature person.
4. I have great confidence in ———'s good judgment.
5. Most people would react favorably to ——— after a brief acquaintance.
6. I think that ——— is one of those people who quickly wins respect.
7. ——— is one of the most likable people I know.
8. ——— is the sort of person whom I myself would like to be.
9. It seems to me that it is very easy for ——— to gain admiration.

rather than liking and loving. The next step, therefore, was to test the scales out, in the context of ongoing dating relationships.

LOVE'S CORRELATES

My subjects for this trial run were 182 dating couples at the University of Michigan.* The modal couple consisted of a junior man and a sopho-

* By 1968–1969, when I conducted the study, it had already become somewhat outmoded for college students to "date." Continuing and casual contacts between the sexes, often facilitated by residential proximity in apartments or dormitories, have to a large extent replaced the traditional pattern in which boy phones girl days or weeks in advance to invite her to a movie, football game, or fraternity party. In spite of the decline of the date, however, exclusive or semi-exclusive relationships between unmarried men and women still thrive on American campuses. One of the major functions of these relationships, although it is not universally subscribed to, continues to be the selection of marriage partners. For lack of a better word ("opposite-sex relationships" is too pedantic; "boy-girl relationships," too patronizing), I continue to refer to these liaisons as "dating relationships" and to the principals as "dating couples."

more woman who had been dating for about one year. Some of the couples had been going together for as long as six or seven years, however, while others had been dating for only a few weeks. About 20 percent of the couples reported that they were engaged.

During the sessions, boyfriends and girlfriends were asked not to sit near one another. Each partner filled out the questionnaire individually. They were assured that their responses would be kept confidential, and that their partners would not be given access to their responses. The questionnaire included the love and liking scales, to be completed first with respect to one's partner and later with respect to a close same-sex friend. In each case the respondent indicated how much he agreed or disagreed with each item by placing a check on the continuous scale. For example:

1. I feel that I can confide in ——— about virtually everything.

Not at all true; disagree completely	Moderately true; agree to some extent	Definitely true; agree completely

With the help of a clear plastic ruler these responses were later converted to numbers from 1 to 9, to be used in analyzing the data. The questionnaire also called for a variety of other pieces of information about the subjects and their relationships, which I will say more about as I present some results.

The statistical analysis of the questionnaire data began with an examination of the internal structure of the liking and love scales. As desired, each of the two scales proved to be internally consistent; that is, in each case its component items were highly intercorrelated. Also in accord with my starting assumption, the correlation between liking and loving scores was only moderate. The correlation between men's love and liking scores for their girlfriends was .56, and the correlation between women's love and liking scores for their boyfriends was .36.*

Although the general pattern of intrascale versus interscale correlations emerged as I had hoped it would, the finding that love and liking were more highly related to one another among men than among women was unexpected. It is possible that this difference is a consequence of the distinctive specializations of the two sexes. In most societies, men tend to be the task specialists, while women tend to be the social–emotional specialists. By virtue of their specialization in matters involving inter-

* The size of the correlation between any two measures indicates how closely people's relative standing on the first measure corresponds to their relative standing on the second. A correlation of 1.00 indicates a perfect correspondence, while a correlation of 0 indicates that the two measures are totally unrelated. Increasing values of a correlation from 0 to 1 indicates increasing degrees of correspondence between the two measures. As a rough rule of thumb we can consider correlations smaller than .30 to be "small," those between .30 and .70 to be "moderate," and those of .70 or greater to be "large."

personal feelings, women may develop a more finely tuned and more discriminating set of interpersonal sentiments than men do. Whereas men may often blur such fine distinctions as the one between liking and loving, women may be more likely to experience and express the two sentiments as being distinct from one another.

Further insight into the nature of liking and loving for the two sexes was derived from a comparison of their average love and liking scores for their dating partners and their same-sex friends. These averages are presented in Table 2. Unsurprisingly, the students reported loving their partners much more than their friends, while the gap between liking for partners and liking for friends was narrower. Less obvious and more informative are the comparisons between the scores of men and women. As Table 2 reveals, the average love scores of men for their girlfriends and of women for their boyfriends were virtually identical. But women *liked* their boyfriends significantly more than they were liked in return. This result seems to reflect contemporary sex roles and stereotypes. The liking scale is "sex-biased" in that it asks the respondent to size up his partner on such stereotypically male characteristics as maturity, intelligence, and good judgment. It asks whether the respondent would recommend the partner for a responsible job. It seems, in other words, to be getting at a task-related sort of liking. It is doubtful that the men in our sample were in fact more responsible, more intelligent, or endowed with better judgment than their girlfriends. Nevertheless, it is generally considered to be more appropriate for men than for women to excel on these dimensions, and the obtained results conform precisely to these cultural expectations.

TABLE 2
AVERAGE LOVE AND LIKING SCORES FOR DATING PARTNERS AND SAME-SEX FRIENDS

	Women	*Men*
Love for partner	90.57	90.44
Liking for partner	89.10	85.30
Love for friend	64.79	54.47
Liking for friend	80.21	78.38

Table 2 also shows that when respondents evaluated their same-sex friends, there was no tendency for men to be liked more than women. Thus, the data do not support the conclusion that men are generally more "likable" than women, but only that they are liked more in the context of dating relationships. The pattern of liking scores suggests that the dating relationship, instead of obliterating stereotypical differences between the sexes, may in fact perpetuate them by emphasizing role and status discrepancies. This pattern is in accord with the feminist critique of traditionally structured male-female relationships as fortifying the favored position of the male and reemphasizing the subservient position of the female.

An additional finding shown in Table 2 is that women tended to love their same-sex friends more than men did. It is indeed more common for female friends than for male friends to speak of themselves as "loving" one another, a linguistic fact that may reflect substantive differences in the nature of men's and women's same-sex friendships. Evidence from several surveys suggests that while women do not typically have more same-sex friends than men, women's friendships tend to be more intimate, involving more spontaneous joint activities and more exchanging of confidences.[7] Men's special difficulties in establishing intimate relationships with other men are underlined by the love-scale results. The male role, for all its task-related "likability," may limit the ability to love.[8] Loving for men may often be channeled into a single opposite-sex relationship, whereas women may be more able to experience and express attachment, caring, and intimacy in other relationships as well.

Another approach toward assessing the validity of the love and liking scales was to examine their correlations with other measures. One of the items included on the questionnaire was "Would you say that you and ________ are in love?" to be answered by circling "yes," "no," or "uncertain." Slightly over two-thirds of both men and women answered affirmatively, with only about 10 percent of each sex reporting that they were not in love and the remaining 22 percent of each sex pleading uncertainty. The correlations between love scores and this "in love" index were reasonably high: .61 for women and .53 for men. The correlations between liking scores and the "in love" index were considerably lower: .29 for women and .36 for men. Thus, the love scale, even though it nowhere includes the word "love" itself, tapped a sentiment that was distinctively related to the students' own categorization of their relationships.

The partners were also asked to estimate the likelihood they would eventually marry one another, on a probability scale ranging from 0 to 100 percent. The average estimate by women was about 50 percent and by men 45 percent. The correlations between love scores and estimates of marriage likelihood were substantial: .60 for women and .59 for men. The correlations between liking scores and marriage likelihood estimates were much lower: .33 for women and .35 for men. Once again the obtained pattern of correlations is reasonable. In societies like our own with a "love pattern" of mate selection, the link between love and marriage is

[7] Studies comparing women's and men's same-sex friendships include Elizabeth Douvan and Joseph Adelson, *The Adolescent Experience* (New York: Wiley, 1966), chap. 6; and Alan Booth, "Sex and Social Participation," *American Sociological Review*, 1972, *37*, 183–192.

[8] For insights into these limitations of the male role, see Joseph Pleck and Jack Sawyer (Eds.), *Men and Masculinity* (Englewood Cliffs, N.J.: Prentice-Hall, Inc., Spectrum Books, 1974).

strongly emphasized by parents, mass media, and other socializing agents. The link between liking and marriage, on the other hand, is too often a well-kept secret. In the next phase of my study I proceeded to put the love scale to a more difficult test, going beyond the questionnaire to direct observations of couples' behavior.

THE GLANCE OF EYE TO EYE

It is well-known folk wisdom that people who are in love spend inordinate amounts of time gazing into each others' eyes. Not all such truisms are in fact true, but there is reason to believe that this one may be. Sociologists and song-writers alike have noted that eye contact plays, as Erving Goffman puts it, "a special role in the communication life of the community.[9] This is because eye contact serves as a mutually understood signal that the communication channel between two people is open. Georg Simmel eloquently described sociological function of eye contact in his *Soziologie*:

> The union and interaction of individuals is based upon mutual glances. This is perhaps the purest and most direct reciprocity that exists anywhere. . . . So tenacious and subtle is this union that it can only be maintained by the shortest and straightest line between the eyes, and the smallest deviation from it, the slightest glance aside, completely destroys the unique character of this union. . . . The totality of social relations of human beings, their self-assertion and self-abnegation, their intimacies and estrangements, would be changed in unpredictable ways if there existed no glance of eye to eye. This mutual glance between persons, in distinction from the simple sight or observation of the other, signifies a wholly new and unique union between them.[10]

Social scientists have speculated about the developmental and evolutionary origins of the social functions of eye contact. One developmental psychologist concluded, for example, that "not physical, but visual contact is at the basis of human sociability." [11] Another reported that "the nature of the eye contact between a mother and her baby seems to cut across all interactional systems and conveys the intimacy or 'distance' characteristic of their relationship as a whole." [12] On the evolutionary level Konrad Lorenz has, in his characteristic analogical style, noted con-

[9] Erving Goffman, *Behavior in Public Places* (New York: Free Press, 1963), p. 92.

[10] Georg Simmel, *Soziologie,* as cited in Robert E. Park and Ernest W. Burgess, *Introduction to the Science of Sociology,* 2d ed. (Chicago: University of Chicago Press, 1924), p. 358.

[11] Harriet L. Rheingold, "The Effect of Environmental Stimulation upon Social and Exploratory Behavior in the Human Infant," in B. M. Foss (Ed.), *Determinants of Infant Behavior,* vol. 1 (New York: Wiley, 1961).

[12] Kenneth S. Robson, "The Role of Eye-to-Eye Contact in Maternal–infant Attachment," *Journal of Child Psychology and Psychiatry,* 1967, *8,* 13–25.

vergences between the functions of eye contact among humans and among lower animals:

> As he makes his proposal, the male [jackdaw] glances continually toward his love but ceases his efforts immediately if she chances to fly away; this however she is not likely to do if she is interested in her admirer. . . . He casts glowing glances straight into his loved one's eyes, while she apparently turns her eyes in all directions other than that of her ardent suitor. In reality, of course, she is watching him all the time, and her quick glances of a fraction of a second are quite long enough to make her realize that all his antics are calculated to inspire her admiration: long enough to let "him" know that "she" knows.[13]

Whatever its origins, eye contact provides a channel through which intimate feelings can be directly expressed. Conversely, when two people do not feel close to one another, eye contact at close quarters is extremely difficult to sustain.

To test the prediction that love and eye contact would be positively related, I invited dating couples who had previously completed the questionnaire to take part in a laboratory experiment. While the two partners sat across a table from one another, waiting for the experiment to begin, they were observed through a one-way mirror by two assistants. Whenever the man looked at the woman's face, one observer, strategically stationed behind the woman, pressed a button that activated a clock recorder. Whenever the woman looked at the man's face, the second observer pushed a button that activated a second clock recorder. Whenever the two observers were pushing their buttons simultaneously, a third clock recorder was activated. The third clock provided the most important of the measures obtained, because it indicated the amount of *simultaneous* looking engaged in by the two partners.

To provide the clearest test of my prediction, I included in the laboratory session only those couples in which both partners were "strong lovers" (both had scored above the median on the love scale) or in which both were "weak lovers" (both had scored below the median). The results indicated that the "strong love" couples indeed made significantly more eye contact than the "weak love" couples did. This finding was certainly not a surprising one. But it added considerably to my confidence that the love scale measured something that went beyond mere questionnaire-checking. Importantly, the difference between "strong love" and "weak love" couples did not emerge with respect to the sheer quantity of looking-at-the-other by the two partners, as recorded on the first and second clocks, but only with respect to mutual eye contact, as recorded on the third clock. "Weak love" boyfriends and girlfriends were as likely as "strong love" partners to look at one another unilaterally, but "strong love" boyfriends and girlfriends were more likely to look at one another simultaneously.

[13] Konrad Lorenz, *King Solomon's Ring* (New York: Crowell, 1952), pp. 156–157.

Eye contact was also measured in two additional experimental conditions. These conditions again compared "strong lovers" and "weak lovers," but the subjects were paired with *other people's* boyfriends and girlfriends rather than with their own partners. These conditions were included to take into account the possibility that "strong lovers" are the sort of people who find it easy to maintain eye contact not only with their partners, but with other people in general. Such a possibility is suggested by Erich Fromm's analysis of love. "Love is not primarily a relationship toward a particular person," Fromm maintains. "It is . . . an *orientation of character* which determines the relatedness of a person toward the world as a whole, not toward one 'object' of love. . . . If I truly love one person I love all persons, I love the world, I love life." [14] Thus one might conjecture that when two "strong lovers" encounter one another, even though they have never before met, they still might find it relatively easy to communicate intimately and to sustain considerable eye contact. Two "weak lovers," on the other hand, might find such intimacy much harder to achieve.

The obtained data did not support this suggestion, however. When the dyads consisted of opposite-sex strangers, the "strong lovers" did not make significantly more eye contact than the "weak lovers." Thus, the pattern of results was more congruent with a conception of love as an attitude toward a particular person than as an orientation toward all mankind. There may still be considerable truth in Fromm's analysis. As codified in Eleanor of Aquitaine's Court of Love, "the man in love becomes accustomed to performing many services gracefully for everyone." [15] But the behavioral implications of this conception of love may be offset by the equally compelling truth that when two people are in love with one another, they have fewer emotional resources left for others. Freud wrote, "The more [two people] are in love, the more completely they suffice for one another." [16] Or, as the popular song has it, "I only have eyes for you."

* * *

Further research involving the love scale is reported in Zick Rubin, *Liking and Loving: An Invitation to Social Psychology* (New York: Holt, Rinehart and Winston, 1973), Chapter 10.

[14] Fromm, pp. 38–39.

[15] Andreas Capellanus, *The Art of Courtly Love,* trans. by John Jay Parry (New York: Columbia University Press, 1941).

[16] Sigmund Freud, "Group Psychology and the Analysis of the Ego," in *The Standard Edition of the Complete Psychological Works of Sigmund Freud,* vol. 18 (London: Hogarth, 1955), p. 140.

EPILOGUE: DOING AND UNDOING

Attempts to specify the forces that affect human behavior are sometimes on the ground that such specifications help to make people into puppets, pulled by strings that are beyond their control. The papers in this collection indeed attest to the impact of powerful external forces upon our social behavior. Our behavior is determined to a large degree by the roles that we are taught, the desires and expectations of others, and the situations into which we are placed. The loneliness of a person uprooted from his neighborhood, the decisions of political leaders, the obedience of experimental subjects, the "apathy" of witnesses of emergencies, and even our choices of husbands and wives have all been shown to be in large measure the products of such external forces. These external forces always interact with internal ones—our individual needs, traits, and values—in determining our reactions. To a large extent, however, like the prisoners and guards in the "Stanford County Prison," we seem fated to play the roles into which we are cast, even if the roles are limiting or demeaning.

But such fatalism is not the message to be obtained from the explorations presented in this book. To the contrary, a systematic understanding of the ways in which people do unto others is a prerequisite for individuals' intelligent attempts to alter these ways. We should recognize, first, that we are not only the molded ones but also the molders. The expectations, roles, and institutions that shape people's behavior and attitudes are themselves created by people. Thus an understanding of the ways in which this control is exerted can also spur us to change it. As Henley suggests, for example, "Men who wish to divest themselves of 'foreskin privilege' can begin to monitor their own acts toward others and their reactions to others' acts, in an attempt to exorcise the subtle power indicators from their daily interactions." Educators who have been made aware (by Rosenthal and Jacobson) of the ways in which teachers' expectations can affect their pupils' intellectual development can act, if they so choose, to eliminate the self-fulfilling prophecies created by "tracking" systems. Similarly, officials whose consciousness of the dehumanizing effects of prisons have been raised by the research of Zimbardo and his colleagues may be prompted to take steps to change these arrangements—for example, by introducing opportunities for prisoners and guards to "rap" and interact as equals.

A better understanding of the social forces that affect us can also point to specific ways in which we can resist these forces. For example, Kanter's analysis of the sources of instability in newly formed communes led her to suggest the value of clearly defined norms and rituals to help pull the commune together as a group. Janis's analysis of policy-making groups resulted in several valuable suggestions for combatting groupthink—for example, assigning one group member to the role of devil's advocate, with the responsibility of airing views that oppose the group's preliminary consensus.

In other cases, the awareness of the way we are affected by others may in itself help us to overcome these forces. Latané and Darley's demonstration that we may be less likely to help a victim when many other people are present may prompt us to take special steps to correct for this tendency. Milgram's dramatic evidence of our willingness to obey the destructive commands of "legitimate authorities" may itself help to diminish that willingness.

In still other cases, an understanding of the social determinants of individual feelings and reactions can help us to cope with these feelings. Research has shown that people can tolerate physical pain more easily when its nature and causes are clearly understood.[1] Similarly, the insight into the causes of loneliness provided by Schachter's and Weiss's research may itself serve to reduce people's distress at times of isolation or loss. And the insights into the nature and determinants of romantic love provided by recent investigations may help people to define their feelings toward one another more clearly. Students participating in my own research have often commented that their participation, which involved completing questionnaires about their relationships, was valuable in clarifying their feelings. One student wrote, for example, "From the beginning, this study has shown me how much of an ass I am at times, how vain I can be, and how much I love (___)."

All of these "enlightenment effects" may have the consequence of making currently accepted social-psychological principles obsolete, since by reacting to the results of research we in effect change them.[2] But whereas such obsolescence may frustrate those among us who seek universal and

[1] For example, Ervin Staub and Deborah S. Kellett, "Increasing pain tolerance by information about aversive stimuli," *Journal of Personality and Social Psychology*, 1972, *2*, 198–203.

[2] Kenneth J. Gergen, "Social psychology as history," *Journal of Personality and Social Psychology*, 1973, *26*, 309–320.

immutable truths, it is in fact the goal of many students of social behavior. There is always a sense in which we remain puppets, pulled by strings that are beyond our control. But as Peter Berger has written: "Unlike puppets, we have the possibility of stopping our movements, looking up and perceiving the machinery by which we have been moved. In this act lies the first step toward freedom." [3]

[3] Peter L. Berger, *Invitation to Sociology: A Humanistic Perspective,* (Garden City, N.Y.: Anchor Books, 1963), p. 176.

Notes on Contributors

SOLOMON E. ASCH is Professor of Psychology at the University of Pennsylvania. Perhaps best known for his ground-breaking research on impressions of personality and on conformity to group pressure, he is also the author of *Social Psychology* (1952).

W. CURTIS BANKS is Assistant Professor of Psychology at Princeton University. His research focuses on person perception, interpersonal influence, and self-concept and achievement in blacks.

JOHN M. DARLEY is Professor of Psychology at Princeton University. He conducts research on helping behavior, aggression, and conformity, and is co-author of *The Unresponsive Bystander: Why Doesn't He Help?* (1970).

CARL H. FELLNER is Professor of Psychiatry and Behavioral Sciences at the University of Washington School of Medicine. From 1957 to 1972 he was on the faculty of the University of Wisconsin Medical School.

WILLIAM J. GOODE is Professor of Sociology at Columbia University. His books include *After Divorce* (1956), *World Revolution and Family Patterns* (1963), and *Explorations in Social Theory* (1973).

CRAIG HANEY is a Russell Sage Foundation Resident in Law and Social Science. His research concerns the interrelatedness of self- and social control processes, and the dehumanizing effects of institutionalization.

NANCY M. HENLEY is Assistant Professor of Psychology at the University of Lowell (Mass.). She is co-editor of *Language and Sex: Difference and Dominance* (1975), and is writing a book on the politics of nonverbal communication.

LENORE JACOBSON holds a doctorate in education and is the principal of the Ponderosa School in South San Francisco. She is co-author of *Pygmalion in the Classroom* (1968).

DAVID JAFFE was an undergraduate psychology major at the time of the Stanford Prison Study. He is currently a student at the University of Chicago Pritzker School of Medicine.

IRVING L. JANIS is Professor of Psychology at Yale University. His books include *Psychological Stress* (1958), *Stress and Frustration* (1971), and *Victims of Groupthink* (1972).

ROSABETH MOSS KANTER is Associate Professor of Sociology at Brandeis University. She is the author of *Commitment and Community* (1972) and editor of *Communes: Creating and Managing the Collective Life* (1973).

BIBB LATANÉ is Professor of Psychology at the Ohio State University. He conducts experimental studies of social behavior among both humans and rats, and is co-author of *The Unresponsive Bystander: Why Doesn't He Help?* (1970).

JOHN R. MARSHALL is Associate Professor and Director of Residency Training in Psychiatry at the University of Wisconsin Medical School. His interests have centered on psychiatric consultation with renal patients.

STANLEY MILGRAM is Professor of Psychology at the Graduate Center of the City University of New York. He is co-author of *Television and Antisocial Behavior* (1973) and author of *Obedience to Authority* (1974).

ROBERT ROSENTHAL is Professor of Social Psychology at Harvard University. His books include *Experimenter Effects in Behavioral Research* (1966), *Pygmalion in the Classroom* (co-author, 1968) and *The Volunteer Subject* (co-author, 1974).

ZICK RUBIN is Lecturer on Social Psychology at Harvard University. He is the author of *Liking and Loving: An Invitation to Social Psychology* (1973) and is General Editor of the Spectrum Books Patterns of Social Behavior series.

STANLEY SCHACHTER is Robert Johnston Niven Professor of Social Psychology at Columbia University. His books include *Social Pressures in Informal Groups* (co-author, 1950), *The Psychology of Affiliation* (1959), and *Emotion, Obesity, and Crime* (1971).

ELAINE WALSTER is Professor of Sociology at the University of Wisconsin. She is the co-author of *Interpersonal Attraction* (1969) and of *Equity Theory* (forthcoming).

ROBERT S. WEISS is Professor of Sociology at the University of Massachusetts, Boston, and a member of the Laboratory of Community Psychiatry, Harvard Medical School. His books include *Loneliness* (1973), *The First Year of Bereavement* (co-author, 1974), and *Marital Separation* (forthcoming).

PHILIP G. ZIMBARDO is Professor of Psychology at Stanford University. His books include *The Cognitive Control of Motivation* (1969), *Influencing Attitudes and Changing Behavior* (co-author, 1969), and *Psychology and Life* (co-author, 1971).